THE VBSCRIPT CODE WARRIOR

Working with ADO

By Richard Thomas Edwards

CONTENTS

Working With ADO 5

Coding Conventions 15

Tables and Views 18

ASP CODE 21

ASPX Code 35

HTA Code 47

HTML CODE 59

Delimited Files 70

    Colon Delimited Horizontal View 71

    Colon Delimited Vertical View 71

    Comma Delimited Horizontal 72

    Comma Delimited Vertical 73

    Exclamation Delimited Horizontal 74

    Exclamation Delimited Vertical 74

    Semi Colon Delimited Horizontal 75

    Semi Colon Delimited Vertical 76

    Tab Delimited Horizontal 77

    Tab Delimited Vertical 78

    Tilde Delimited Horizontal 78

    Tilde Delimited Vertical 79

XML Files 81
    Attribute XML Using A Text file 81
    Attribute XML Using the DOM 82
    Element XML Using A Text file 83
    Element XML Using the DOM 83
    Element XML FOR XSL Using A Text File 84
    Element XML FOR XSL Using The DOM 85
    Schema XML Using A Text File 86
    Schema XML Using the DOM 87
Excel Coding Examples 88
    Excel Code in Horizontal Format using a CSV File 88
    Excel Code in Vertical Format using a CSV File 89
    Excel using Horizontal Format Automation Code 90
    Excel using Vertical Format Automation Code 90
    Excel Spreadsheet Example 91
Creating XSL Files 96
    Single Line Horizontal Reports 97
    Multi Line Horizontal Reports 99
    Single Line Vertical Reports 102
    Multi Line Vertical Reports 104
    Single Line Horizontal Tables 107
    Multi Line Horizontal Tables 109
    Single Line Vertical Tables 112
    Multi Line Vertical Tables 114
Stylesheets 117

None 118

Its A Table 118

Black and White Text 122

Colored Text 124

Oscillating Row Colors 127

Ghost Decorated 129

3D 131

Shadow Box 137

Working With ADO
Making working with ADO easy

The hardest part of working with ADO looking for help on the web and none of it makes sense.
—Richard Thomas Edwards

Have you found this to be true: You go up to the web, type in a couple of key words and a whole lot of "not even close" results popup. Even the ones that look promising, are a piece of the whole puzzle and doesn't make it easy for you to compare what you may have been able to do already with what you need to do next. Well you've come to the right place to get the steps down and help you make your Python experience with ADO a pleasure instead of a pain and a frustrating run around. There are four principle parts to working with ADO.

1. The connection must be made to a local or remote database that is either physical or is running as a service.
2. The version of a physical database must be known.
3. You must determine whether the database requires a username or password to connect to it.
4. You need to know the name of the table you want to use to return data from.

Yes, it can get much more complex than that. You may have to create some complex queries. Things like joins and stored procedures may be on your radar but right now, let's just get you connected.

The first object you want to create is the ADODB.Connection. There is also something that will help you make it visually easier to do all of this. This is what you do:

```
Set cn = CreateObject("ADODB.Connection")
Set dl = CreateObject("DataLinks")
Set cn = dl.PromptNew()
WScript.Echo(cn.connectionstring)
```

Copy the code from here, open notepad and save the file as "Datakinks.vbs" – yes, the quotes are required. Then run it by clicking on the icon that got produced as a Python file.

This code will produce this:

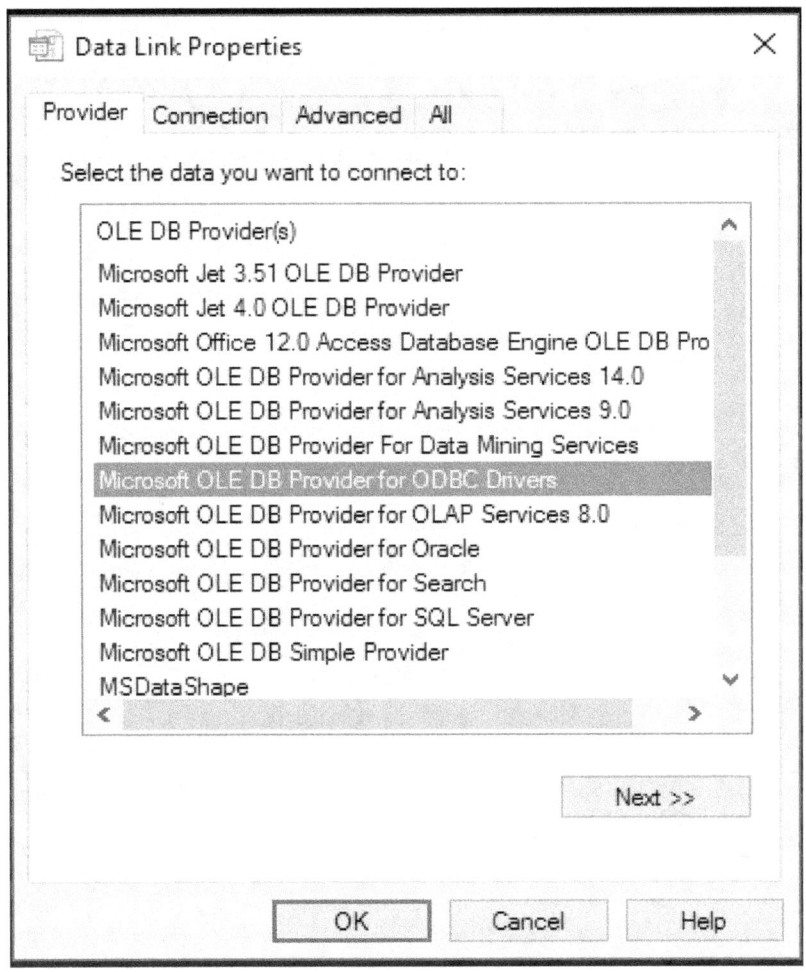

Let's suppose I know I want to connect to an older database. One with a .mdb extension. If I click on the Microsoft.Jet.OLEDB.4.0 and then click on the connection tab and then click on the search button:

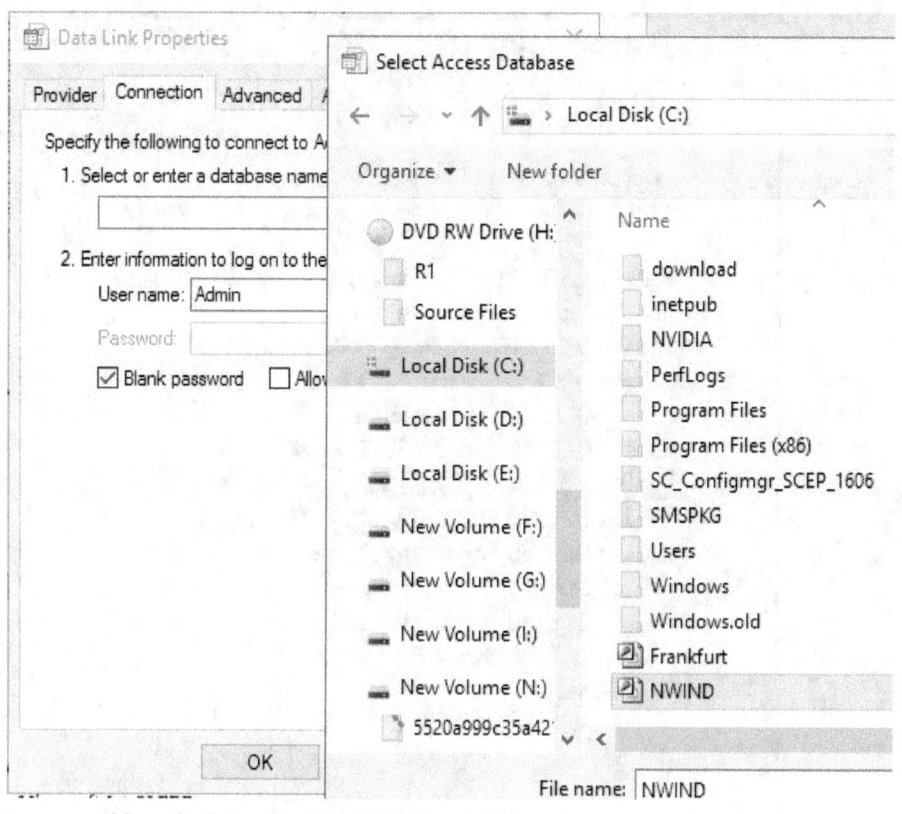

I am ten able to look for the file, click okay and:

Now, I'm ready to test the connection. And when I click on Test connection:

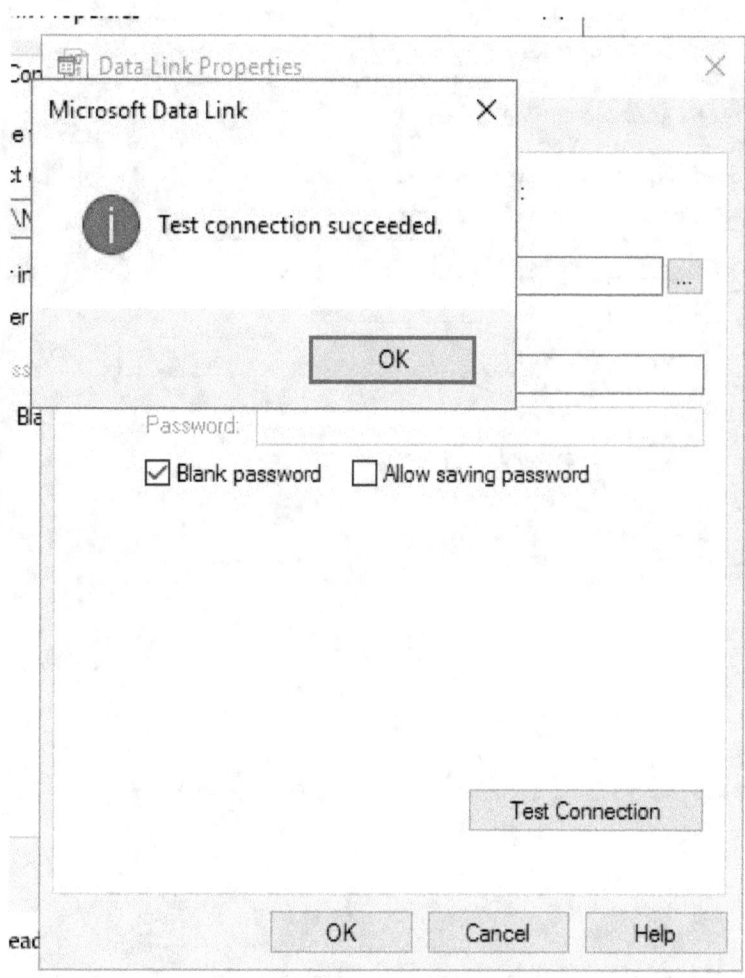

And when you close this all down, your connection string would be:

Provider=Microsoft.Jet.OLEDB.4.0;Data Source=C:\NWIND.MDB;Persist Security Info=False

What about if you already have a connection String and want to test it

Set cn = CreateObject("ADODB.Connection")
cn.Provider="Microsoft.Jet.OLEDB.4.0"

cn.Properties("Data Source").Value = "C:\\NWIND.MDB"
Set dl = CreateObject("DataLinks")
dl.PromptEdit(cn)
WScript.Echo(cn.connectionstring)

After you've cleared the semi-colon right after the mdb and when you click on Test Connection.

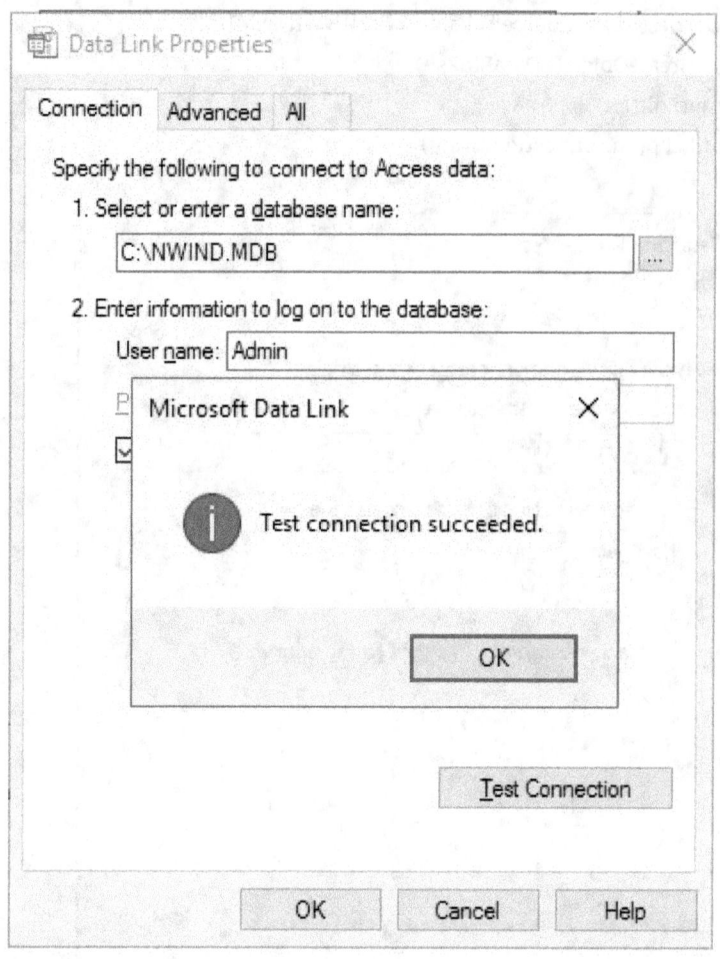

And it returns:

Provider=Microsoft.Jet.OLEDB.4.0;Data Source="C:\NWIND.MDB;"

HOW CONNECTION STRINGS WORK

So, what is a connection string?

A connection string is a Set of properties you put together on a single line that tells the connection, command or Recordset what provider, driver or ISAM to use and where to look for the database.

Here's pretty much, the classical connection string:

Provider=Microsoft.Jet.OLEDB.4.0;Data Source=C:\NWIND.MDB;Persist Security Info=False

ADO is an acronym for Active-X Data Objects. In VBSCRIPT, you can use it to connect to both the 32-bit and 64-bit versions of Providers, Drivers and ISAMS

The reason why ADO came about in the first place was because DAO relied a lot on disk drives to do most of the work and disk drives were extremely slow.

It is also what was used to build the .Net ODBC, OLEDB, Oracle Client and SQL Client components. So, everything you do in ADO can be applied to the various .Net world as well. Therefore, if you learn ADO, the others are self-explanatory and a walk in the park.

This toolkit includes:
- ADODB.Connection
- ADODB.Command
- ADODB.Recordset

While I love working with SQL Server, I use it in its simplest of terms. I create a connection string cnstr and then a strQuery as my SQL query string.

Here' how these combinations have been worked with in the past:
- Connection, Command and Recordset
- Connection and Recordset
- Command and Recordset
- Recordset

Most of my experiences deal with these four conventions although I have used the ADODB.STREAM with XML and ADSI.

Coding Conventions

Below, are the ways you will find the ADODB.Connection, ADODB.Command and ADODB.Recordset used today. Just remember that they are not scribed in cement and there is more than one way to get the connection to work.

Alternative connection one:

```
Set cn = CreateObject("ADODB.Connection")
cn.Provider="Microsoft.Jet.OLEDB.4.0"
cn.Properties("Data Source").Value = "C:\\NWIND.MDB"
```

Alternative connection two:

```
Set cn = CreateObject("ADODB.Connection")
cn.Open("Microsoft.Jet.OLEDB.4.0;Data Source = "C:\\NWIND.MDB")
```

Connection, Command and Recordset

```
Set cn = CreateObject("ADODB.Connection")
Set cmd = CreateObject("ADODB.Command")
```

```
Set rs = CreateObject("ADODB.Recordset")

cn.ConnectionString = cnstr
cn.Open()

cmd.ActiveConnection = cn
cmd.CommandType=1
cmd.CommandText = "Select * From (Products)"
cmd.Execute()

rs.CursorLocation = 3
rs.LockType = 3
rs.Open(cmd)

rs.MoveFirst()
```

Connection and Recordset

```
Set cn = CreateObject("ADODB.Connection")
Set rs = CreateObject("ADODB.Recordset")
cn.ConnectionString = cnstr
cn.Open()

rs.ActiveConnection = cn
rs.CursorLocation = 3
rs.LockType = 3
rs.Open("Select * From (Products)")

rs.MoveFirst()
```

Command and Recordset

```
Set cmd = CreateObject("ADODB.Command")
Set rs = CreateObject("ADODB.Recordset")

cmd.ActiveConnection = cnstr
cmd.CommandType=1
cmd.CommandText = "Select * From (Products)"
cmd.Execute()

rs.CursorLocation = 3
rs.LockType = 3
rs.Open(cmd)

rs.MoveFirst()
```

Recordset

```
Set rs = CreateObject("ADODB.Recordset")
rs.ActiveConnection = cnstr
rs.CursorLocation = 3
rs.LockType = 3
rs.Open("Select * From (Products)")

rs.MoveFirst()
```

Tables and Views

At this point you're probably scratching your head trying to figure out how I went from creating a query against a known table. Well aside from the fact that I do know this because I've use that database for lots of examples over the years, I also know that cn.OpenSchema works with the Microsoft.Jet.OleDb.4.0 provider and that the value is 20.

```
Set cn = CreateObject("ADODB.Connection")
Set rs = CreateObject("ADODB.Recordset")
cn.Provider="Microsoft.Jet.OLEDB.4.0"
cn.Properties("Data Source").Value = "C:\\NWIND.MDB"
cn.Open()

Set rs = cn.OpenSchema(20)
Do While rs.EOF = false
   if rs.Fields("TABLE_TYPE").Value = "TABLE" then
      WScript.Echo(str(rs.Fields("TABLE_NAME").Value))
   End If
   rs.MoveNext()
Loop
```
The Results:

Categories

Customers

> **Employees**
> **Order Details**
> **Orders**
> **Products**
> **Shippers**
> **Suppliers**

As for Views:

```
Set cn = CreateObject("ADODB.Connection")
Set rs = CreateObject("ADODB.Recordset")
cn.Provider="Microsoft.Jet.OLEDB.4.0"
cn.Properties("Data Source").Value = "C:\\NWIND.MDB"
cn.Open()

Set rs = cn.OpenSchema(20)
Do While rs.EOF = false
   if rs.Fields("TABLE_TYPE").Value = "VIEW" then
      WScript.Echo(str(rs.Fields("TABLE_NAME").Value))
   End If
   rs.MoveNext()
Loop
```

The Results:

> **Category Sales for 1995**
> **Current Product List**
> **Invoices**
> **Order Details Extended**
> **Order Subtotals**
> **Product Sales for 1995**

Products Above Average Price
Quarterly Orders
Sales by Category
Ten Most Expensive Products

A few words of caution here. The Schema types are provider specific, so don't expect the same syntax I just used with the Microsoft.Jet.OLEDB.4.0 provider if you are using the SQL Server or Oracle provider. Not only will the Schema Type be different so will the field names be different, too.

Okay, so now you know something about connection strings and how to get table and view information, it is time to start using that information to create an assortment of user outputs which just might make you and your boss get some warm and fuzzy feelings.

ASP CODE

THERE IS NOTING FANTASIC ABOUT CREATING ASP OR ASPX WEB PAGES. In fact, additional hoops must be jumped - web site where you can cut and paste what you just created from here is one of them. So, with that said, I've added enough bells and whistles into the code structure to make it worth your while.

Here's what is in store for you:

- Report View
  - Horizontal
    - None
    - Button
    - Combobox
    - Div
    - Link
    - Listbox
    - Span
    - Textarea
    - Textbox
  - Vertical
    - None
    - Button
    - Combobox
    - Div
    - Link
    - Listbox

- - - Span
    - Textarea
    - Textbox
- Table View
  - Horizontal
    - None
    - Button
    - Combobox
    - Div
    - Link
    - Listbox
    - Span
    - Textarea
    - Textbox
  - Vertical
    - None
    - Button
    - Combobox
    - Div
    - Link
    - Listbox
    - Span
    - Textarea
    - Textbox

```
Set ws = CreateObject("WScript.Shell")
Set fso = CreateObject("Scripting.FileSystemObject")
Set txtstream =fso.OpenTextFile(ws.CurrentDirectory + "\Products.asp", 2, true, -2)
txtstream.WriteLine("<html>")
txtstream.WriteLine("<head>")
txtstream.WriteLine("<title>" + Tablename + "</title>")
#Add Stylesheet here
txtstream.WriteLine("<body>")
txtstream.WriteLine("</br>")
```

Horizontal Reports

```
txtstream.WriteLine("<table border=0 cellspacing=3 cellpadding=3>")
txtstream.WriteLine("<%")
txtstream.WriteLine("Response.Write(""<tr>""" + vbcrlf)")
For x = 0 to rs.Fields.Count-1
    txtstream.WriteLine("Response.Write(""<th style="" font-family:Calibri, Sans-Serif;font-size: 12px;color:darkred;"" align='left' nowrap='nowrap'>"" + rs.Fields(x).Name + ""</th>""" + vbcrlf)")
Next
txtstream.WriteLine("Response.Write(""</tr>""" + vbcrlf)")
Do While(rs.EOF = false)
   txtstream.WriteLine("Response.Write(""<tr>""" + vbcrlf)")
   For x = 0 to rs.Fields.Count-1
```

NONE

txtstream.WriteLine("Response.Write(""<td style=""font-family:Calibri, Sans-Serif;font-size: 12px;color:navy;"" align='left' nowrap='nowrap'>" + rs.Fields(x).Value + "</td>"" + vbcrlf)")

Button

txtstream.WriteLine("Response.Write(""<td style=""font-family:Calibri, Sans-Serif;font-size: 12px;color:navy;"" align='left' nowrap='true'><button style='width:100%;' value ='" + rs.Fields(x).Value + "'>" + rs.Fields(x).Value + "</button></td>"" + vbcrlf)")

COMBOBOX

txtstream.WriteLine("Response.Write(""<td style=""font-family:Calibri, Sans-Serif;font-size: 12px;color:navy;"" align='left' nowrap='true'><select><option value = """" + rs.Fields(x).Value + """">" + rs.Fields(x).Value + "</option></select></td>"" + vbcrlf)")

DIV

txtstream.WriteLine("Response.Write(""<td style=""font-family:Calibri, Sans-Serif;font-size: 12px;color:navy;"" align='left' nowrap='true'> " + rs.Fields(x).Value + " </td>"" + vbcrlf)")

LINK

txtstream.WriteLine("Response.Write(""<td style=""font-family:Calibri, Sans-Serif;font-size: 12px;color:navy;"" align='left' nowrap='true'><a href='" + rs.Fields(x).Value + "'>" + rs.Fields(x).Value + "</a></td>"" + vbcrlf)")

LISTBOX

```
            txtstream.WriteLine("Response.Write(""<td        style=""""font-family:Calibri,    Sans-Serif;font-size:    12px;color:navy;""""    align='left' nowrap='true'><select multiple><option value = """" + rs.Fields(x).Value + """">" + rs.Fields(x).Value + "</option></select></td>"""" + vbcrlf)")
```

SPAN

```
            txtstream.WriteLine("Response.Write(""<td        style=""""font-family:Calibri,    Sans-Serif;font-size:    12px;color:navy;""""    align='left' nowrap='true'><span>" + rs.Fields(x).Value + "</span></td>"""" + vbcrlf)")
```

TEXTAREA

```
            txtstream.WriteLine("Response.Write(""<td        style=""""font-family:Calibri,    Sans-Serif;font-size:    12px;color:navy;""""    align='left' nowrap='true'><textarea>" + rs.Fields(x).Value + "</textarea></td>"""" + vbcrlf)")
```

TEXTBOX

```
            txtstream.WriteLine("Response.Write(""<td        style=""""font-family:Calibri,    Sans-Serif;font-size:    12px;color:navy;""""    align='left' nowrap='true'><input    type=text    value=""""" + rs.Fields(x).Value + """""></input></td>"""" + vbcrlf)")
        Next
        txtstream.WriteLine("Response.Write(""</tr>"""" + vbcrlf)")
        rs.MoveNext
    Loop
    txtstream.WriteLine("%>")
    txtstream.WriteLine("</table>")
    txtstream.WriteLine("</body>")
    txtstream.WriteLine("</html>")
    txtstream.Close()
```

Vertical Reports

```
txtstream.WriteLine("<table border=0 cellspacing=3 cellpadding=3>")
txtstream.WriteLine("<%")
For x = 0 to rs.Fields.Count-1
    txtstream.WriteLine("Response.Write(""<tr><th style="""" font-family:Calibri, Sans-Serif;font-size: 12px;color:darkred;"""" align='left' nowrap='nowrap'>" + rs.Fields(x).Name + "</th>""" + vbcrlf)")
    rs.MoveFirst()
    Do While(rs.EOF = false)
        txtstream.WriteLine("Response.Write(""<td style=""""font-family:Calibri, Sans-Serif;font-size: 12px;color:navy;"""">" + rs.Fields(x).Value + "</td>""" + vbcrlf)")
```

NONE

```
        txtstream.WriteLine("Response.Write(""<td style=""""font-family:Calibri, Sans-Serif;font-size: 12px;color:navy;"""" align='left' nowrap='nowrap'>" + rs.Fields(x).Value + "</td>""" + vbcrlf)")
```

Button

```
        txtstream.WriteLine("Response.Write(""<td style=""""font-family:Calibri, Sans-Serif;font-size: 12px;color:navy;"""" align='left' nowrap='true'><button style='width:100%;' value ='" + rs.Fields(x).Value + "'>" + rs.Fields(x).Value + "</button></td>""" + vbcrlf)")
```

Combobox

txtstream.WriteLine("Response.Write(""<td style=""font-family:Calibri, Sans-Serif;font-size: 12px;color:navy;"" align='left' nowrap='true'><select><option value = """ + rs.Fields(x).Value + """>" + rs.Fields(x).Value + "</option></select></td>"" + vbcrlf)")

Div

txtstream.WriteLine("Response.Write(""<td style=""font-family:Calibri, Sans-Serif;font-size: 12px;color:navy;"" align='left' nowrap='true'> " + rs.Fields(x).Value + " </td>"" + vbcrlf)")

Link

txtstream.WriteLine("Response.Write(""<td style=""font-family:Calibri, Sans-Serif;font-size: 12px;color:navy;"" align='left' nowrap='true'><a href='" + rs.Fields(x).Value + "'>" + rs.Fields(x).Value + "</a></td>"" + vbcrlf)")

Listbox

txtstream.WriteLine("Response.Write(""<td style=""font-family:Calibri, Sans-Serif;font-size: 12px;color:navy;"" align='left' nowrap='true'><select multiple><option value = """ + rs.Fields(x).Value + """>" + rs.Fields(x).Value + "</option></select></td>"" + vbcrlf)")

Span

txtstream.WriteLine("Response.Write(""<td style=""font-family:Calibri, Sans-Serif;font-size: 12px;color:navy;"" align='left' nowrap='true'>" + rs.Fields(x).Value + "</td>"" + vbcrlf)")

Textarea

```
            txtstream.WriteLine("Response.Write(""<td    style=""font-family:Calibri, Sans-Serif;font-size: 12px;color:navy;"" align='left' nowrap='true'><textarea>" + rs.Fields(x).Value + "</textarea></td>"" + vbcrlf)")
```

Textbox

```
            txtstream.WriteLine("Response.Write(""<td  style=""font-family:Calibri, Sans-Serif;font-size:   12px;color:navy;""    align='left'   nowrap='true'><input type=text value="""" + rs.Fields(x).Value + """"></input></td>"" + vbcrlf)")
         rs.MoveNext
      loop
         txtstream.WriteLine("Response.Write(""</tr>"" + vbcrlf)")
    Next
    txtstream.WriteLine("%>")
    txtstream.WriteLine("</table>")
    txtstream.WriteLine("</body>")
    txtstream.WriteLine("</html>")
    txtstream.Close()
```

Horizontal Tables

```
    txtstream.WriteLine("<table    style='border:Double;border-width:1px;border-color:navy;' rules=all frames=both cellpadding=2 cellspacing=2 Width=0>")
    txtstream.WriteLine("<%")
    txtstream.WriteLine("Response.Write(""<tr>"" + vbcrlf)")
    For x = 0 to rs.Fields.Count-1
        txtstream.WriteLine("Response.Write(""<th   style=""   font-family:Calibri, Sans-Serif;font-size:  12px;color:darkred;""   align='left'   nowrap='nowrap'>" + rs.Fields(x).Name + "</th>"" + vbcrlf)")
```

Next
    txtstream.WriteLine("Response.Write("""</tr>""" + vbcrlf)")
Do While(rs.EOF = false)
    txtstream.WriteLine("Response.Write("""<tr>""" + vbcrlf)")
        For x = 0 to rs.Fields.Count-1

NONE

txtstream.WriteLine("Response.Write("""<td style=""""font-family:Calibri, Sans-Serif;font-size: 12px;color:navy;"""" align='left' nowrap='nowrap'>" + rs.Fields(x).Value + "</td>""" + vbcrlf)")

Button

txtstream.WriteLine("Response.Write("""<td style=""""font-family:Calibri, Sans-Serif;font-size: 12px;color:navy;"""" align='left' nowrap='true'><button style='width:100%;' value ='" + rs.Fields(x).Value + "'>" + rs.Fields(x).Value + "</button></td>""" + vbcrlf)")

COMBOBOX

txtstream.WriteLine("Response.Write("""<td style=""""font-family:Calibri, Sans-Serif;font-size: 12px;color:navy;"""" align='left' nowrap='true'><select><option value = """" + rs.Fields(x).Value + """">" + rs.Fields(x).Value + "</option></select></td>""" + vbcrlf)")

DIV

txtstream.WriteLine("Response.Write("""<td style=""""font-family:Calibri, Sans-Serif;font-size: 12px;color:navy;"""" align='left' nowrap='true'> " + rs.Fields(x).Value + " </td>""" + vbcrlf)")

LINK

txtstream.WriteLine("Response.Write(""<td style=""font-family:Calibri, Sans-Serif;font-size: 12px;color:navy;"" align='left' nowrap='true'><a href='" + rs.Fields(x).Value + "'>" + rs.Fields(x).Value + "</a></td>""" + vbcrlf)")

LISTBOX

txtstream.WriteLine("Response.Write(""<td style=""font-family:Calibri, Sans-Serif;font-size: 12px;color:navy;"" align='left' nowrap='true'><select multiple><option value = """ + rs.Fields(x).Value + """>" + rs.Fields(x).Value + "</option></select></td>""" + vbcrlf)")

SPAN

txtstream.WriteLine("Response.Write(""<td style=""font-family:Calibri, Sans-Serif;font-size: 12px;color:navy;"" align='left' nowrap='true'>" + rs.Fields(x).Value + "</td>""" + vbcrlf)")

TEXTAREA

txtstream.WriteLine("Response.Write(""<td style=""font-family:Calibri, Sans-Serif;font-size: 12px;color:navy;"" align='left' nowrap='true'><textarea>" + rs.Fields(x).Value + "</textarea></td>""" + vbcrlf)")

TEXTBOX

txtstream.WriteLine("Response.Write(""<td style=""font-family:Calibri, Sans-Serif;font-size: 12px;color:navy;"" align='left'

nowrap='true'><input type=text value=""" + rs.Fields(x).Value + """></input></td>""" + vbcrlf)")

txtstream.WriteLine("Response.Write(""</tr>""" + vbcrlf)")
rs.MoveNext

txtstream.WriteLine("%>")
txtstream.WriteLine("</table>")
txtstream.WriteLine("</body>")
txtstream.WriteLine("</html>")
txtstream.Close()

Vertical Tables

txtstream.WriteLine("<table style='border:Double;border-width:1px;border-color:navy;' rules=all frames=both cellpadding=2 cellspacing=2 Width=0>")

txtstream.WriteLine("<%")

For x = 0 to rs.Fields.Count-1
txtstream.WriteLine("Response.Write(""<tr><th style=""" font-family:Calibri, Sans-Serif;font-size: 12px;color:darkred;""" align='left' nowrap='nowrap'>" + rs.Fields(x).Name + "</th>""" + vbcrlf)")
rs.MoveFirst()
Do While(rs.EOF = false)
txtstream.WriteLine("Response.Write(""<td style=""""font-family:Calibri, Sans-Serif;font-size: 12px;color:navy;"""">" + rs.Fields(x).Value + "</td>""" + vbcrlf)")

NONE

txtstream.WriteLine("Response.Write(""<td style=""font-family:Calibri, Sans-Serif;font-size: 12px;color:navy;"" align='left' nowrap='nowrap'>" + rs.Fields(x).Value + "</td>""" + vbcrlf)")

Button

txtstream.WriteLine("Response.Write(""<td style=""font-family:Calibri, Sans-Serif;font-size: 12px;color:navy;"" align='left' nowrap='true'><button style='width:100%;' value ='" + rs.Fields(x).Value + "'>" + rs.Fields(x).Value + "</button></td>""" + vbcrlf)")

Combobox

txtstream.WriteLine("Response.Write(""<td style=""font-family:Calibri, Sans-Serif;font-size: 12px;color:navy;"" align='left' nowrap='true'><select><option value = """ + rs.Fields(x).Value + """>" + rs.Fields(x).Value + "</option></select></td>""" + vbcrlf)")

Div

txtstream.WriteLine("Response.Write(""<td style=""font-family:Calibri, Sans-Serif;font-size: 12px;color:navy;"" align='left' nowrap='true'> " + rs.Fields(x).Value + " </td>""" + vbcrlf)")

Link

txtstream.WriteLine("Response.Write(""<td style=""font-family:Calibri, Sans-Serif;font-size: 12px;color:navy;"" align='left' nowrap='true'><a href='" + rs.Fields(x).Value + "'>" + rs.Fields(x).Value + "</a></td>""" + vbcrlf)")

Listbox

txtstream.WriteLine("Response.Write(""<td style=""font-family:Calibri, Sans-Serif;font-size: 12px;color:navy;"" align='left' nowrap='true'><select multiple><option value = """ + rs.Fields(x).Value + """>" + rs.Fields(x).Value + "</option></select></td>"" + vbcrlf)")

Span

txtstream.WriteLine("Response.Write(""<td style=""font-family:Calibri, Sans-Serif;font-size: 12px;color:navy;"" align='left' nowrap='true'>" + rs.Fields(x).Value + "</td>"" + vbcrlf)")

Textarea

txtstream.WriteLine("Response.Write(""<td style=""font-family:Calibri, Sans-Serif;font-size: 12px;color:navy;"" align='left' nowrap='true'><textarea>" + rs.Fields(x).Value + "</textarea></td>"" + vbcrlf)")

Textbox

txtstream.WriteLine("Response.Write(""<td style=""font-family:Calibri, Sans-Serif;font-size: 12px;color:navy;"" align='left' nowrap='true'><input type=text value=""" + rs.Fields(x).Value + """></input></td>"" + vbcrlf)")
       rs.MoveNext

txtstream.WriteLine("Response.Write(""</tr>"" + vbcrlf)")

txtstream.WriteLine("%>")
txtstream.WriteLine("</table>")
txtstream.WriteLine("</body>")
txtstream.WriteLine("</html>")
txtstream.Close()

ASPX Code
Chapter Subtitle

*Chapter Epigraph uses a quote or verse to
introduce the chapter and set the stage.*
—*Attribute the quote*

BELOW ARE EXAMPLES OF USING ADO THROUGH VBSCRIPT TO CREATE ASPX FILES.

```
Set ws = CreateObject("WScript.Shell")
Set fso = CreateObject("Scripting.FileSystemObject")
Set txtstream =fso.OpenTextFile(ws.CurrentDirectory + "\Products.asp", 2, true, -2)
txtstream.WriteLine("<html>")
txtstream.WriteLine("<head>")
txtstream.WriteLine("<title>" + Tablename + "</title>")
#Add Stylesheet here
txtstream.WriteLine("<body>")
txtstream.WriteLine("</br>")
```

Horizontal Reports

```
    txtstream.WriteLine("<table border=0 cellspacing=3 cellpadding=3>")
    txtstream.WriteLine("<%")
    txtstream.WriteLine("Response.Write(""<tr>"" + vbcrlf)")
    For x = 0 to rs.Fields.Count-1
        txtstream.WriteLine("Response.Write(""<th style="" font-family:Calibri, Sans-Serif;font-size: 12px;color:darkred;"" align='left' nowrap='nowrap'>"" + rs.Fields(x).Name + ""</th>"" + vbcrlf)")
    Next
    txtstream.WriteLine("Response.Write(""</tr>"" + vbcrlf)")
    Do While(rs.EOF = false)
        txtstream.WriteLine("Response.Write(""<tr>"" + vbcrlf)")
        For x = 0 to rs.Fields.Count-1
```

NONE

```
            txtstream.WriteLine("Response.Write(""<td style=""font-family:Calibri, Sans-Serif;font-size: 12px;color:navy;"" align='left' nowrap='nowrap'>"" + rs.Fields(x).Value + ""</td>"" + vbcrlf)")
```

Button

```
            txtstream.WriteLine("Response.Write(""<td style=""font-family:Calibri, Sans-Serif;font-size: 12px;color:navy;"" align='left' nowrap='true'><button style='width:100%;' value ='"" + rs.Fields(x).Value + ""'>"" + rs.Fields(x).Value + ""</button></td>"" + vbcrlf)")
```

COMBOBOX

txtstream.WriteLine("Response.Write(""<td style=""font-family:Calibri, Sans-Serif;font-size: 12px;color:navy;"" align='left' nowrap='true'><select><option value = """" + rs.Fields(x).Value + """">" + rs.Fields(x).Value + "</option></select></td>"" + vbcrlf)")

DIV

txtstream.WriteLine("Response.Write(""<td style=""font-family:Calibri, Sans-Serif;font-size: 12px;color:navy;"" align='left' nowrap='true'> " + rs.Fields(x).Value + " </td>"" + vbcrlf)")

LINK

txtstream.WriteLine("Response.Write(""<td style=""font-family:Calibri, Sans-Serif;font-size: 12px;color:navy;"" align='left' nowrap='true'><a href='" + rs.Fields(x).Value + "'>" + rs.Fields(x).Value + "</a></td>"" + vbcrlf)")

LISTBOX

txtstream.WriteLine("Response.Write(""<td style=""font-family:Calibri, Sans-Serif;font-size: 12px;color:navy;"" align='left' nowrap='true'><select multiple><option value = """" + rs.Fields(x).Value + """">" + rs.Fields(x).Value + "</option></select></td>"" + vbcrlf)")

SPAN

txtstream.WriteLine("Response.Write(""<td style=""font-family:Calibri, Sans-Serif;font-size: 12px;color:navy;"" align='left' nowrap='true'>" + rs.Fields(x).Value + "</td>"" + vbcrlf)")

TEXTAREA

txtstream.WriteLine("Response.Write(""<td style=""font-family:Calibri, Sans-Serif;font-size: 12px;color:navy;"" align='left' nowrap='true'><textarea>" + rs.Fields(x).Value + "</textarea></td>"" + vbcrlf)")

TEXTBOX

txtstream.WriteLine("Response.Write(""<td style=""font-family:Calibri, Sans-Serif;font-size: 12px;color:navy;"" align='left' nowrap='true'><input type=text value=""" + rs.Fields(x).Value + """></input></td>"" + vbcrlf)")

```
    Next
    txtstream.WriteLine("Response.Write(""</tr>"" + vbcrlf)")
    rs.MoveNext
Loop
txtstream.WriteLine("%>")
txtstream.WriteLine("</table>")
txtstream.WriteLine("</body>")
txtstream.WriteLine("</html>")
txtstream.Close()
```

Vertical Reports

txtstream.WriteLine("<table border=0 cellspacing=3 cellpadding=3>")
txtstream.WriteLine("<%")
For x = 0 to rs.Fields.Count-1

txtstream.WriteLine("Response.Write(""<tr><th style="" font-family:Calibri, Sans-Serif;font-size: 12px;color:darkred;"" align='left' nowrap='nowrap'>" + rs.Fields(x).Name + "</th>"" + vbcrlf)")

  rs.MoveFirst()

  Do While(rs.EOF = false)

txtstream.WriteLine("Response.Write(""<td style=""font-family:Calibri, Sans-Serif;font-size: 12px;color:navy;"">" + rs.Fields(x).Value + "</td>"" + vbcrlf)")

NONE

txtstream.WriteLine("Response.Write(""<td style=""font-family:Calibri, Sans-Serif;font-size: 12px;color:navy;"" align='left' nowrap='nowrap'>" + rs.Fields(x).Value + "</td>"" + vbcrlf)")

Button

txtstream.WriteLine("Response.Write(""<td style=""font-family:Calibri, Sans-Serif;font-size: 12px;color:navy;"" align='left' nowrap='true'><button style='width:100%;' value ='" + rs.Fields(x).Value + "'>" + rs.Fields(x).Value + "</button></td>"" + vbcrlf)")

Combobox

txtstream.WriteLine("Response.Write(""<td style=""font-family:Calibri, Sans-Serif;font-size: 12px;color:navy;"" align='left' nowrap='true'><select><option value = """ + rs.Fields(x).Value + """>" + rs.Fields(x).Value + "</option></select></td>"" + vbcrlf)")

Div

txtstream.WriteLine("Response.Write(""<td style=""font-family:Calibri, Sans-Serif;font-size: 12px;color:navy;"" align='left' nowrap='true'> " + rs.Fields(x).Value + " </td>"" + vbcrlf)")

Link

txtstream.WriteLine("Response.Write(""<td style=""font-family:Calibri, Sans-Serif;font-size: 12px;color:navy;"" align='left' nowrap='true'><a href='" + rs.Fields(x).Value + "'>" + rs.Fields(x).Value + "</a></td>"" + vbcrlf)")

Listbox

txtstream.WriteLine("Response.Write(""<td style=""font-family:Calibri, Sans-Serif;font-size: 12px;color:navy;"" align='left' nowrap='true'><select multiple><option value = """ + rs.Fields(x).Value + """>" + rs.Fields(x).Value + "</option></select></td>"" + vbcrlf)")

Span

txtstream.WriteLine("Response.Write(""<td style=""font-family:Calibri, Sans-Serif;font-size: 12px;color:navy;"" align='left' nowrap='true'>" + rs.Fields(x).Value + "</td>"" + vbcrlf)")

Textarea

txtstream.WriteLine("Response.Write(""<td style=""font-family:Calibri, Sans-Serif;font-size: 12px;color:navy;"" align='left' nowrap='true'><textarea>" + rs.Fields(x).Value + "</textarea></td>"" + vbcrlf)")

Textbox

```
            txtstream.WriteLine("Response.Write(""<td  style=""font-family:Calibri,
Sans-Serif;font-size:   12px;color:navy;""    align='left'    nowrap='true'><input
type=text value=""" + rs.Fields(x).Value + """></input></td>"" + vbcrlf)")
            rs.MoveNext
        Loop
        txtstream.WriteLine("Response.Write(""</tr>"" + vbcrlf)")
    Next
    txtstream.WriteLine("%>")
    txtstream.WriteLine("</table>")
    txtstream.WriteLine("</body>")
    txtstream.WriteLine("</html>")
    txtstream.Close()
```

Horizontal Tables

```
    txtstream.WriteLine("<table    style='border:Double;border-width:1px;border-
color:navy;' rules=all frames=both cellpadding=2 cellspacing=2 Width=0>")
    txtstream.WriteLine("<%")
    txtstream.WriteLine("Response.Write(""<tr>"" + vbcrlf)")
    For x = 0 to rs.Fields.Count-1
        txtstream.WriteLine("Response.Write(""<th   style=""  font-family:Calibri,
Sans-Serif;font-size:  12px;color:darkred;""    align='left'  nowrap='nowrap'>"  +
rs.Fields(x).Name + "</th>"" + vbcrlf)")
    Next
    txtstream.WriteLine("Response.Write(""</tr>"" + vbcrlf)")
    Do While(rs.EOF = false)
        txtstream.WriteLine("Response.Write(""<tr>"" + vbcrlf)")
        For x = 0 to rs.Fields.Count-1
```

NONE

txtstream.WriteLine("Response.Write(""<td style=""font-family:Calibri, Sans-Serif;font-size: 12px;color:navy;"" align='left' nowrap='nowrap'>" + rs.Fields(x).Value + "</td>"" + vbcrlf)")

Button

txtstream.WriteLine("Response.Write(""<td style=""font-family:Calibri, Sans-Serif;font-size: 12px;color:navy;"" align='left' nowrap='true'><button style='width:100%;' value ='" + rs.Fields(x).Value + "'>" + rs.Fields(x).Value + "</button></td>"" + vbcrlf)")

COMBOBOX

txtstream.WriteLine("Response.Write(""<td style=""font-family:Calibri, Sans-Serif;font-size: 12px;color:navy;"" align='left' nowrap='true'><select><option value = """" + rs.Fields(x).Value + """">" + rs.Fields(x).Value + "</option></select></td>"" + vbcrlf)")

DIV

txtstream.WriteLine("Response.Write(""<td style=""font-family:Calibri, Sans-Serif;font-size: 12px;color:navy;"" align='left' nowrap='true'> " + rs.Fields(x).Value + " </td>"" + vbcrlf)")

LINK

txtstream.WriteLine("Response.Write(""<td style=""font-family:Calibri, Sans-Serif;font-size: 12px;color:navy;"" align='left' nowrap='true'><a href='" + rs.Fields(x).Value + "'>" + rs.Fields(x).Value + "</a></td>"" + vbcrlf)")

LISTBOX

txtstream.WriteLine("Response.Write(""<td style=""font-family:Calibri, Sans-Serif;font-size: 12px;color:navy;"" align='left' nowrap='true'><select multiple><option value = """ + rs.Fields(x).Value + """>" + rs.Fields(x).Value + "</option></select></td>"" + vbcrlf)")

SPAN

txtstream.WriteLine("Response.Write(""<td style=""font-family:Calibri, Sans-Serif;font-size: 12px;color:navy;"" align='left' nowrap='true'>" + rs.Fields(x).Value + "</td>"" + vbcrlf)")

TEXTAREA

txtstream.WriteLine("Response.Write(""<td style=""font-family:Calibri, Sans-Serif;font-size: 12px;color:navy;"" align='left' nowrap='true'><textarea>" + rs.Fields(x).Value + "</textarea></td>"" + vbcrlf)")

TEXTBOX

txtstream.WriteLine("Response.Write(""<td style=""font-family:Calibri, Sans-Serif;font-size: 12px;color:navy;"" align='left' nowrap='true'><input type=text value=""" + rs.Fields(x).Value + """></input></td>"" + vbcrlf)")
    Next
    txtstream.WriteLine("Response.Write(""</tr>"" + vbcrlf)")
    rs.MoveNext
Loop
txtstream.WriteLine("%>")
txtstream.WriteLine("</table>")
txtstream.WriteLine("</body>")
txtstream.WriteLine("</html>")

txtstream.Close()

Vertical Tables

txtstream.WriteLine("<table style='border:Double;border-width:1px;border-color:navy;' rules=all frames=both cellpadding=2 cellspacing=2 Width=0>")
txtstream.WriteLine("<%")
For x = 0 to rs.Fields.Count-1
    txtstream.WriteLine("Response.Write(""<tr><th style="" font-family:Calibri, Sans-Serif;font-size: 12px;color:darkred;"" align='left' nowrap='nowrap'>" + rs.Fields(x).Name + "</th>"" + vbcrlf)")
    rs.MoveFirst()
    Do While rs.EOF = false
        txtstream.WriteLine("Response.Write(""<td style=""font-family:Calibri, Sans-Serif;font-size: 12px;color:navy;"">" + rs.Fields(x).Value + "</td>"" + vbcrlf)")

NONE

    txtstream.WriteLine("Response.Write(""<td style=""font-family:Calibri, Sans-Serif;font-size: 12px;color:navy;"" align='left' nowrap='nowrap'>" + rs.Fields(x).Value + "</td>"" + vbcrlf)")

Button

    txtstream.WriteLine("Response.Write(""<td style=""font-family:Calibri, Sans-Serif;font-size: 12px;color:navy;"" align='left' nowrap='true'><button style='width:100%;' value ='" + rs.Fields(x).Value + "'>" + rs.Fields(x).Value + "</button></td>"" + vbcrlf)")

Combobox

txtstream.WriteLine("Response.Write(""<td style=""font-family:Calibri, Sans-Serif;font-size: 12px;color:navy;"" align='left' nowrap='true'><select><option value = """ + rs.Fields(x).Value + """>" + rs.Fields(x).Value + "</option></select></td>"" + vbcrlf)")

Div

txtstream.WriteLine("Response.Write(""<td style=""font-family:Calibri, Sans-Serif;font-size: 12px;color:navy;"" align='left' nowrap='true'> " + rs.Fields(x).Value + " </td>"" + vbcrlf)")

Link

txtstream.WriteLine("Response.Write(""<td style=""font-family:Calibri, Sans-Serif;font-size: 12px;color:navy;"" align='left' nowrap='true'><a href='" + rs.Fields(x).Value + "'>" + rs.Fields(x).Value + "</a></td>"" + vbcrlf)")

Listbox

txtstream.WriteLine("Response.Write(""<td style=""font-family:Calibri, Sans-Serif;font-size: 12px;color:navy;"" align='left' nowrap='true'><select multiple><option value = """ + rs.Fields(x).Value + """>" + rs.Fields(x).Value + "</option></select></td>"" + vbcrlf)")

Span

txtstream.WriteLine("Response.Write(""<td style=""font-family:Calibri, Sans-Serif;font-size: 12px;color:navy;"" align='left' nowrap='true'>" + rs.Fields(x).Value + "</td>"" + vbcrlf)")

Textarea

txtstream.WriteLine("Response.Write(""<td style=""font-family:Calibri, Sans-Serif;font-size: 12px;color:navy;"" align='left' nowrap='true'><textarea>" + rs.Fields(x).Value + "</textarea></td>"" + vbcrlf)")

Textbox

txtstream.WriteLine("Response.Write(""<td style=""font-family:Calibri, Sans-Serif;font-size: 12px;color:navy;"" align='left' nowrap='true'><input type=text value=""" + rs.Fields(x).Value + """></input></td>"" + vbcrlf)")
      rs.MoveNext
  loop
  txtstream.WriteLine("Response.Write(""</tr>"" + vbcrlf)")
next
txtstream.WriteLine("%>")
txtstream.WriteLine("</table>")
txtstream.WriteLine("</body>")
txtstream.WriteLine("</html>")
txtstream.Close()

HTA Code
Chapter Subtitle

*Chapter Epigraph uses a quote or verse to
introduce the chapter and set the stage.*
—*Attribute the quote*

LIKE ASP AND ASPX, HTA BEEN AROUND FOR SOME TIME NOW. Despite the fact the concept appears to be old or outdated You should know that it is still being used as HTML as an EXE.

```
Set ws = CreateObject("WScript.Shell")
Set fso = CreateObject("Scripting.FileSystemObject")
Set txtstream =fso.OpenTextFile(ws.CurrentDirectory + "\Products.hta", 2, true, -2)
    txtstream.WriteLine("<html>")
    txtstream.WriteLine("<head>")
    txtstream.WriteLine("<HTA:APPLICATION ")
    txtstream.WriteLine("ID = ""Products"" ")
    txtstream.WriteLine("APPLICATIONNAME = ""Products"" ")
    txtstream.WriteLine("SCROLL = ""yes"" ")
```

```
txtstream.WriteLine("SINGLEINSTANCE = ""yes"" ")
txtstream.WriteLine("WINDOWSTATE = ""maximize"" >")
txtstream.WriteLine("<title>" + Tablename + "</title>")
#Add Stylesheet here
txtstream.WriteLine("<body>")
txtstream.WriteLine("</br>")
```

Horizontal Reports

```
txtstream.WriteLine("<table border=0 cellspacing=3 cellpadding=3>")
txtstream.WriteLine("<tr>")
For x = 0 to rs.Fields.Count-1
    txtstream.WriteLine("<th style="" font-family:Calibri, Sans-Serif;font-size: 12px;color:darkred;""  align='left'  nowrap='nowrap'>" + rs.Fields(x).Name + "</th>")
Next
txtstream.WriteLine("</tr>")
Do While(rs.EOF = false)
   txtstream.WriteLine("<tr>")
   For x = 0 to rs.Fields.Count-1
```

NONE

```
       txtstream.WriteLine("<td style=""font-family:Calibri, Sans-Serif;font-size: 12px;color:navy;""  align='left'  nowrap='nowrap'>" + rs.Fields(x).Value + "</td>")
```

Button

txtstream.WriteLine("<td style=""font-family:Calibri, Sans-Serif;font-size: 12px;color:navy;"" align='left' nowrap='true'><button style='width:100%;' value ='" + rs.Fields(x).Value + "'>" + rs.Fields(x).Value + "</button></td>")

COMBOBOX

txtstream.WriteLine("<td style=""font-family:Calibri, Sans-Serif;font-size: 12px;color:navy;"" align='left' nowrap='true'><select><option value = """" + rs.Fields(x).Value + """">" + rs.Fields(x).Value + "</option></select></td>")

DIV

txtstream.WriteLine("<td style=""font-family:Calibri, Sans-Serif;font-size: 12px;color:navy;"" align='left' nowrap='true'> " + rs.Fields(x).Value + " </td>")

LINK

txtstream.WriteLine("<td style=""font-family:Calibri, Sans-Serif;font-size: 12px;color:navy;"" align='left' nowrap='true'><a href='" + rs.Fields(x).Value + "'>" + rs.Fields(x).Value + "</a></td>")

LISTBOX

txtstream.WriteLine("<td style=""font-family:Calibri, Sans-Serif;font-size: 12px;color:navy;"" align='left' nowrap='true'><select multiple><option value = """" + rs.Fields(x).Value + """">" + rs.Fields(x).Value + "</option></select></td>")

SPAN

txtstream.WriteLine("<td style=""font-family:Calibri, Sans-Serif;font-size: 12px;color:navy;"" align='left' nowrap='true'>" + rs.Fields(x).Value + "</td>")

TEXTAREA

```
            txtstream.WriteLine("<td style=""font-family:Calibri, Sans-Serif;font-size: 12px;color:navy;"" align='left' nowrap='true'><textarea>" + rs.Fields(x).Value + "</textarea></td>")
```

TEXTBOX

```
            txtstream.WriteLine("<td style=""font-family:Calibri, Sans-Serif;font-size: 12px;color:navy;"" align='left' nowrap='true'><input type=text value=""" + rs.Fields(x).Value + """></input></td>")
        Next
        txtstream.WriteLine("</tr>")
        rs.MoveNext
    Loop
    txtstream.WriteLine("</table>")
    txtstream.WriteLine("</body>")
    txtstream.WriteLine("</html>")
    txtstream.Close()
```

Vertical Reports

```
    txtstream.WriteLine("<table border=0 cellspacing=3 cellpadding=3>")
    For x = 0 to rs.Fields.Count-1
        txtstream.WriteLine("<tr><th style="" font-family:Calibri, Sans-Serif;font-size: 12px;color:darkred;"" align='left' nowrap='nowrap'>" + rs.Fields(x).Name + "</th>")
        rs.MoveFirst()
        Do While(rs.EOF = false)
```

txtstream.WriteLine("<td style=""font-family:Calibri, Sans-Serif;font-size: 12px;color:navy;"">" + rs.Fields(x).Value + "</td>")

NONE

txtstream.WriteLine("<td style=""font-family:Calibri, Sans-Serif;font-size: 12px;color:navy;"" align='left' nowrap='nowrap'>" + rs.Fields(x).Value + "</td>")

Button

txtstream.WriteLine("<td style=""font-family:Calibri, Sans-Serif;font-size: 12px;color:navy;"" align='left' nowrap='true'><button style='width:100%;' value ='" + rs.Fields(x).Value + "'>" + rs.Fields(x).Value + "</button></td>")

Combobox

txtstream.WriteLine("<td style=""font-family:Calibri, Sans-Serif;font-size: 12px;color:navy;"" align='left' nowrap='true'><select><option value = '""" + rs.Fields(x).Value + """'>" + rs.Fields(x).Value + "</option></select></td>")

Div

txtstream.WriteLine("<td style=""font-family:Calibri, Sans-Serif;font-size: 12px;color:navy;"" align='left' nowrap='true'> " + rs.Fields(x).Value + " </td>")

Link

```
            txtstream.WriteLine("<td style=""font-family:Calibri, Sans-Serif;font-size: 12px;color:navy;"" align='left' nowrap='true'><a href='" + rs.Fields(x).Value + "'>" + rs.Fields(x).Value + "</a></td>")
```

Listbox

```
            txtstream.WriteLine("<td style=""font-family:Calibri, Sans-Serif;font-size: 12px;color:navy;"" align='left' nowrap='true'><select multiple><option value = """ + rs.Fields(x).Value + """>" + rs.Fields(x).Value + "</option></select></td>")
```

Span

```
            txtstream.WriteLine("<td style=""font-family:Calibri, Sans-Serif;font-size: 12px;color:navy;"" align='left' nowrap='true'><span>" + rs.Fields(x).Value + "</span></td>")
```

Textarea

```
            txtstream.WriteLine("<td style=""font-family:Calibri, Sans-Serif;font-size: 12px;color:navy;"" align='left' nowrap='true'><textarea>" + rs.Fields(x).Value + "</textarea></td>")
```

Textbox

```
            txtstream.WriteLine("<td style=""font-family:Calibri, Sans-Serif;font-size: 12px;color:navy;"" align='left' nowrap='true'><input type=text value=""" + rs.Fields(x).Value + """></input></td>")
        rs.MoveNext
    Loop
    txtstream.WriteLine("</tr>")
Next
txtstream.WriteLine("</table>")
```

```
txtstream.WriteLine("</body>")
txtstream.WriteLine("</html>")
txtstream.Close()
```

Horizontal Tables

```
txtstream.WriteLine("<table     style='border:Double;border-width:1px;border-color:navy;' rules=all frames=both cellpadding=2 cellspacing=2 Width=0>")
txtstream.WriteLine("<tr>")
For x = 0 to rs.Fields.Count-1
   txtstream.WriteLine("<th style="" font-family:Calibri, Sans-Serif;font-size: 12px;color:darkred;""   align='left'   nowrap='nowrap'>" + rs.Fields(x).Name + "</th>")
Next
txtstream.WriteLine("</tr>")
Do While(rs.EOF = false)
   txtstream.WriteLine("<tr>")
      For x = 0 to rs.Fields.Count-1
```

NONE

```
         txtstream.WriteLine("<td style=""font-family:Calibri, Sans-Serif;font-size: 12px;color:navy;""   align='left'   nowrap='nowrap'>" + rs.Fields(x).Value + "</td>")
```

Button

txtstream.WriteLine("<td style=""font-family:Calibri, Sans-Serif;font-size: 12px;color:navy;"" align='left' nowrap='true'><button style='width:100%;' value ='" + rs.Fields(x).Value + "'>" + rs.Fields(x).Value + "</button></td>")

COMBOBOX

txtstream.WriteLine("<td style=""font-family:Calibri, Sans-Serif;font-size: 12px;color:navy;"" align='left' nowrap='true'><select><option value = """ + rs.Fields(x).Value + """>" + rs.Fields(x).Value + "</option></select></td>")

DIV

txtstream.WriteLine("<td style=""font-family:Calibri, Sans-Serif;font-size: 12px;color:navy;"" align='left' nowrap='true'> " + rs.Fields(x).Value + " </td>")

LINK

txtstream.WriteLine("<td style=""font-family:Calibri, Sans-Serif;font-size: 12px;color:navy;"" align='left' nowrap='true'><a href='" + rs.Fields(x).Value + "'>" + rs.Fields(x).Value + "</a></td>")

LISTBOX

txtstream.WriteLine("<td style=""font-family:Calibri, Sans-Serif;font-size: 12px;color:navy;"" align='left' nowrap='true'><select multiple><option value = """ + rs.Fields(x).Value + """>" + rs.Fields(x).Value + "</option></select></td>")

SPAN

txtstream.WriteLine("<td style=""font-family:Calibri, Sans-Serif;font-size: 12px;color:navy;"" align='left' nowrap='true'>" + rs.Fields(x).Value + "</td>")

TEXTAREA

```
        txtstream.WriteLine("<td style=""font-family:Calibri, Sans-Serif;font-size: 12px;color:navy;"" align='left' nowrap='true'><textarea>" + rs.Fields(x).Value + "</textarea></td>")
```

TEXTBOX

```
        txtstream.WriteLine("<td style=""font-family:Calibri, Sans-Serif;font-size: 12px;color:navy;"" align='left' nowrap='true'><input type=text value=""" + rs.Fields(x).Value + """></input></td>")
      Next
      txtstream.WriteLine("</tr>")
      rs.MoveNext
    Loop
    txtstream.WriteLine("</table>")
    txtstream.WriteLine("</body>")
    txtstream.WriteLine("</html>")
    txtstream.Close()
```

Vertical Tables

```
    txtstream.WriteLine("<table style='border:Double;border-width:1px;border-color:navy;' rules=all frames=both cellpadding=2 cellspacing=2 Width=0>")
      For x = 0 to rs.Fields.Count-1
        txtstream.WriteLine("<tr><th style="" font-family:Calibri, Sans-Serif;font-size: 12px;color:darkred;"" align='left' nowrap='nowrap'>" + rs.Fields(x).Name + "</th>")
        rs.MoveFirst()
        Do While rs.EOF = false
```

txtstream.WriteLine("<td style=""font-family:Calibri, Sans-Serif;font-size: 12px;color:navy;"">" + rs.Fields(x).Value + "</td>")

NONE

txtstream.WriteLine("<td style=""font-family:Calibri, Sans-Serif;font-size: 12px;color:navy;"" align='left' nowrap='nowrap'>" + rs.Fields(x).Value + "</td>")

Button

txtstream.WriteLine("<td style=""font-family:Calibri, Sans-Serif;font-size: 12px;color:navy;"" align='left' nowrap='true'><button style='width:100%;' value ='" + rs.Fields(x).Value + "'>" + rs.Fields(x).Value + "</button></td>")

Combobox

txtstream.WriteLine("<td style=""font-family:Calibri, Sans-Serif;font-size: 12px;color:navy;"" align='left' nowrap='true'><select><option value = """ + rs.Fields(x).Value + """>" + rs.Fields(x).Value + "</option></select></td>")

Div

txtstream.WriteLine("<td style=""font-family:Calibri, Sans-Serif;font-size: 12px;color:navy;"" align='left' nowrap='true'> " + rs.Fields(x).Value + " </td>")

Link

```
        txtstream.WriteLine("<td  style=""font-family:Calibri, Sans-Serif;font-size:
12px;color:navy;"" align='left' nowrap='true'><a href='" + rs.Fields(x).Value + "'>"
+ rs.Fields(x).Value + "</a></td>")
```

Listbox

```
        txtstream.WriteLine("<td  style=""font-family:Calibri, Sans-Serif;font-size:
12px;color:navy;"" align='left' nowrap='true'><select multiple><option value = """"
+ rs.Fields(x).Value + """>" + rs.Fields(x).Value + "</option></select></td>")
```

Span

```
        txtstream.WriteLine("<td  style=""font-family:Calibri, Sans-Serif;font-
size: 12px;color:navy;"" align='left' nowrap='true'><span>" + rs.Fields(x).Value
+ "</span></td>")
```

Textarea

```
        txtstream.WriteLine("<td  style=""font-family:Calibri, Sans-Serif;font-size:
12px;color:navy;"" align='left' nowrap='true'><textarea>" + rs.Fields(x).Value +
"</textarea></td>")
```

Textbox

```
        txtstream.WriteLine("<td  style=""font-family:Calibri, Sans-Serif;font-
size: 12px;color:navy;"" align='left' nowrap='true'><input type=text value="""" +
rs.Fields(x).Value + """></input></td>")
            rs.MoveNext
        Loop
        txtstream.WriteLine("</tr>")
    Next
    txtstream.WriteLine("</table>")
```

```
txtstream.WriteLine("</body>")
txtstream.WriteLine("</html>")
txtstream.Close()
```

HTML CODE

WHAT CAN I SAY ABOUT HTML5 AND CSS THAT HASN'T BEEN SAID ALREADY? Well, I can say that it has come a long way since the 1990s.

```
Set ws = CreateObject("WScript.Shell")
Set fso = CreateObject("Scripting.FileSystemObject")
Set txtstream =fso.OpenTextFile(ws.CurrentDirectory + "\Products.html", 2, true, -2)
    txtstream.WriteLine("<html>")
    txtstream.WriteLine("<head>")
    txtstream.WriteLine("<title>" + Tablename + "</title>")
    #Add Stylesheet here
    txtstream.WriteLine("<body>")
    txtstream.WriteLine("</br>")
```

Horizontal Reports

```
    txtstream.WriteLine("<table border=0 cellspacing=3 cellpadding=3>")
```

```
txtstream.WriteLine("<tr>")
For x = 0 to rs.Fields.Count-1
    txtstream.WriteLine("<th style="""" font-family:Calibri, Sans-Serif;font-size: 12px;color:darkred;"""  align='left'  nowrap='nowrap'>" + rs.Fields(x).Name + "</th>")

    txtstream.WriteLine("</tr>")
Next
Do While(rs.EOF = false)
    txtstream.WriteLine("<tr>")
    For x = 0 to rs.Fields.Count-1
```

NONE

```
txtstream.WriteLine("<td style=""""font-family:Calibri, Sans-Serif;font-size: 12px;color:navy;"""  align='left'  nowrap='nowrap'>" + rs.Fields(x).Value + "</td>")
```

Button

```
txtstream.WriteLine("<td style=""""font-family:Calibri, Sans-Serif;font-size: 12px;color:navy;"""  align='left'  nowrap='true'><button style='width:100%;' value ='" + rs.Fields(x).Value + "'>" + rs.Fields(x).Value + "</button></td>")
```

COMBOBOX

```
txtstream.WriteLine("<td style=""""font-family:Calibri, Sans-Serif;font-size: 12px;color:navy;"""  align='left'  nowrap='true'><select><option value = """ + rs.Fields(x).Value + """">" + rs.Fields(x).Value + "</option></select></td>")
```

DIV

txtstream.WriteLine("<td style=""font-family:Calibri, Sans-Serif;font-size: 12px;color:navy;"" align='left' nowrap='true'> " + rs.Fields(x).Value + " </td>")

LINK

txtstream.WriteLine("<td style=""font-family:Calibri, Sans-Serif;font-size: 12px;color:navy;"" align='left' nowrap='true'><a href='" + rs.Fields(x).Value + "'>" + rs.Fields(x).Value + "</a></td>")

LISTBOX

txtstream.WriteLine("<td style=""font-family:Calibri, Sans-Serif;font-size: 12px;color:navy;"" align='left' nowrap='true'><select multiple><option value = """" + rs.Fields(x).Value + """">" + rs.Fields(x).Value + "</option></select></td>")

SPAN

txtstream.WriteLine("<td style=""font-family:Calibri, Sans-Serif;font-size: 12px;color:navy;"" align='left' nowrap='true'>" + rs.Fields(x).Value + "</td>")

TEXTAREA

txtstream.WriteLine("<td style=""font-family:Calibri, Sans-Serif;font-size: 12px;color:navy;"" align='left' nowrap='true'><textarea>" + rs.Fields(x).Value + "</textarea></td>")

TEXTBOX

```
        txtstream.WriteLine("<td style=""font-family:Calibri, Sans-Serif;font-size: 12px;color:navy;"" align='left' nowrap='true'><input type=text value=""" + rs.Fields(x).Value + """></input></td>")
    Next
    txtstream.WriteLine("</tr>")
    rs.MoveNext
Loop
txtstream.WriteLine("</table>")
txtstream.WriteLine("</body>")
txtstream.WriteLine("</html>")
txtstream.Close()
```

Vertical Reports

```
txtstream.WriteLine("<table border=0 cellspacing=3 cellpadding=3>")
For x = 0 to rs.Fields.Count-1
    txtstream.WriteLine("<tr><th style="" font-family:Calibri, Sans-Serif;font-size: 12px;color:darkred;"" align='left' nowrap='nowrap'>" + rs.Fields(x).Name + "</th>")
    rs.MoveFirst()
    Do While(rs.EOF = false)
        txtstream.WriteLine("<td style=""font-family:Calibri, Sans-Serif;font-size: 12px;color:navy;"">" + rs.Fields(x).Value + "</td>")
```

NONE

```
        txtstream.WriteLine("<td style=""font-family:Calibri, Sans-Serif;font-size: 12px;color:navy;"" align='left' nowrap='nowrap'>" + rs.Fields(x).Value + "</td>")
```

Button

txtstream.WriteLine("<td style=""font-family:Calibri, Sans-Serif;font-size: 12px;color:navy;"" align='left' nowrap='true'><button style='width:100%;' value ='" + rs.Fields(x).Value + "'>" + rs.Fields(x).Value + "</button></td>")

Combobox

txtstream.WriteLine("<td style=""font-family:Calibri, Sans-Serif;font-size: 12px;color:navy;"" align='left' nowrap='true'><select><option value = """ + rs.Fields(x).Value + """>" + rs.Fields(x).Value + "</option></select></td>")

Div

txtstream.WriteLine("<td style=""font-family:Calibri, Sans-Serif;font-size: 12px;color:navy;"" align='left' nowrap='true'> " + rs.Fields(x).Value + " </td>")

Link

txtstream.WriteLine("<td style=""font-family:Calibri, Sans-Serif;font-size: 12px;color:navy;"" align='left' nowrap='true'><a href='" + rs.Fields(x).Value + "'>" + rs.Fields(x).Value + "</a></td>")

Listbox

txtstream.WriteLine("<td style=""font-family:Calibri, Sans-Serif;font-size: 12px;color:navy;"" align='left' nowrap='true'><select multiple><option value = """ + rs.Fields(x).Value + """>" + rs.Fields(x).Value + "</option></select></td>")

Span

txtstream.WriteLine("<td style=""font-family:Calibri, Sans-Serif;font-size: 12px;color:navy;"" align='left' nowrap='true'>" + rs.Fields(x).Value + "</td>")

Textarea

txtstream.WriteLine("<td style=""font-family:Calibri, Sans-Serif;font-size: 12px;color:navy;"" align='left' nowrap='true'><textarea>" + rs.Fields(x).Value + "</textarea></td>")

Textbox

txtstream.WriteLine("<td style=""font-family:Calibri, Sans-Serif;font-size: 12px;color:navy;"" align='left' nowrap='true'><input type=text value=""" + rs.Fields(x).Value + """></input></td>")
    rs.MoveNext
  Loop
  txtstream.WriteLine("</tr>")
Next
txtstream.WriteLine("</table>")
txtstream.WriteLine("</body>")
txtstream.WriteLine("</html>")
txtstream.Close()

Horizontal Tables

txtstream.WriteLine("<table style='border:Double;border-width:1px;border-color:navy;' rules=all frames=both cellpadding=2 cellspacing=2 Width=0>")
  txtstream.WriteLine("<tr>")
  For x = 0 to rs.Fields.Count-1

txtstream.WriteLine("<th style="""" font-family:Calibri, Sans-Serif;font-size: 12px;color:darkred;""" align='left' nowrap='nowrap'>" + rs.Fields(x).Name + "</th>")
   Next
   txtstream.WriteLine("</tr>")
   Do While(rs.EOF = false)
      txtstream.WriteLine("<tr>")
         For x = 0 to rs.Fields.Count-1

NONE

txtstream.WriteLine("<td style=""""font-family:Calibri, Sans-Serif;font-size: 12px;color:navy;"""" align='left' nowrap='nowrap'>" + rs.Fields(x).Value + "</td>")

Button

txtstream.WriteLine("<td style=""""font-family:Calibri, Sans-Serif;font-size: 12px;color:navy;"""" align='left' nowrap='true'><button style='width:100%;' value ='" + rs.Fields(x).Value + "'>" + rs.Fields(x).Value + "</button></td>")

COMBOBOX

txtstream.WriteLine("<td style=""""font-family:Calibri, Sans-Serif;font-size: 12px;color:navy;"""" align='left' nowrap='true'><select><option value = """" + rs.Fields(x).Value + """">" + rs.Fields(x).Value + "</option></select></td>")

DIV

txtstream.WriteLine("<td style=""""font-family:Calibri, Sans-Serif;font-size: 12px;color:navy;"""" align='left' nowrap='true'> " + rs.Fields(x).Value + " </td>")

LINK

txtstream.WriteLine("<td style=""font-family:Calibri, Sans-Serif;font-size: 12px;color:navy;"" align='left' nowrap='true'><a href='" + rs.Fields(x).Value + "'>" + rs.Fields(x).Value + "</a></td>")

LISTBOX

txtstream.WriteLine("<td style=""font-family:Calibri, Sans-Serif;font-size: 12px;color:navy;"" align='left' nowrap='true'><select multiple><option value = """ + rs.Fields(x).Value + """>" + rs.Fields(x).Value + "</option></select></td>")

SPAN

txtstream.WriteLine("<td style=""font-family:Calibri, Sans-Serif;font-size: 12px;color:navy;"" align='left' nowrap='true'>" + rs.Fields(x).Value + "</td>")

TEXTAREA

txtstream.WriteLine("<td style=""font-family:Calibri, Sans-Serif;font-size: 12px;color:navy;"" align='left' nowrap='true'><textarea>" + rs.Fields(x).Value + "</textarea></td>")

TEXTBOX

txtstream.WriteLine("<td style=""font-family:Calibri, Sans-Serif;font-size: 12px;color:navy;"" align='left' nowrap='true'><input type=text value=""" + rs.Fields(x).Value + """></input></td>")
    Next
    txtstream.WriteLine("</tr>")
    rs.MoveNext

```
Loop
txtstream.WriteLine("</table>")
txtstream.WriteLine("</body>")
txtstream.WriteLine("</html>")
txtstream.Close()
```

Vertical Tables

```
    txtstream.WriteLine("<table    style='border:Double;border-width:1px;border-color:navy;' rules=all frames=both cellpadding=2 cellspacing=2 Width=0>")
    For x = 0 to rs.Fields.Count-1
        txtstream.WriteLine("<tr><th   style=""   font-family:Calibri,  Sans-Serif;font-size:   12px;color:darkred;""   align='left'   nowrap='nowrap'>"   +  rs.Fields(x).Name + "</th>")
        rs.MoveFirst()
        Do While rs.EOF = false
            txtstream.WriteLine("<td  style=""font-family:Calibri,  Sans-Serif;font-size: 12px;color:navy;"">" + rs.Fields(x).Value + "</td>")
```

NONE

```
            txtstream.WriteLine("<td  style=""font-family:Calibri,  Sans-Serif;font-size:  12px;color:navy;""   align='left'  nowrap='nowrap'>"  +  rs.Fields(x).Value + "</td>")
```

Button

```
            txtstream.WriteLine("<td  style=""font-family:Calibri,  Sans-Serif;font-size:  12px;color:navy;""   align='left'  nowrap='true'><button  style='width:100%;' value ='" + rs.Fields(x).Value + "'>" + rs.Fields(x).Value + "</button></td>")
```

Combobox

txtstream.WriteLine("<td style=""font-family:Calibri, Sans-Serif;font-size: 12px;color:navy;"" align='left' nowrap='true'><select><option value = """ + rs.Fields(x).Value + """>" + rs.Fields(x).Value + "</option></select></td>")

Div

txtstream.WriteLine("<td style=""font-family:Calibri, Sans-Serif;font-size: 12px;color:navy;"" align='left' nowrap='true'> " + rs.Fields(x).Value + " </td>")

Link

txtstream.WriteLine("<td style=""font-family:Calibri, Sans-Serif;font-size: 12px;color:navy;"" align='left' nowrap='true'><a href='" + rs.Fields(x).Value + "'>" + rs.Fields(x).Value + "</a></td>")

Listbox

txtstream.WriteLine("<td style=""font-family:Calibri, Sans-Serif;font-size: 12px;color:navy;"" align='left' nowrap='true'><select multiple><option value = """ + rs.Fields(x).Value + """>" + rs.Fields(x).Value + "</option></select></td>")

Span

txtstream.WriteLine("<td style=""font-family:Calibri, Sans-Serif;font-size: 12px;color:navy;"" align='left' nowrap='true'>" + rs.Fields(x).Value + "</td>")

Textarea

txtstream.WriteLine("<td style=""font-family:Calibri, Sans-Serif;font-size: 12px;color:navy;"" align='left' nowrap='true'><textarea>" + rs.Fields(x).Value + "</textarea></td>")

Textbox

txtstream.WriteLine("<td style=""font-family:Calibri, Sans-Serif;font-size: 12px;color:navy;"" align='left' nowrap='true'><input type=text value=""" + rs.Fields(x).Value + """></input></td>")
    rs.MoveNext
  Loop
  txtstream.WriteLine("</tr>")
Next
txtstream.WriteLine("</table>")
txtstream.WriteLine("</body>")
txtstream.WriteLine("</html>")
txtstream.Close()

Delimited Files
Chapter Subtitle

*Chapter Epigraph uses a quote or verse to
introduce the chapter and set the stage.*
—Attribute the quote

THERE ARE MANY DIFFERENT KINDS OF DELIMITED FILES. The ones we are going to be using are the most common ones. And by Common, this will include:

- Colon Delimited
- Comma Delimited
- Exclamation Delimited
- Semi-Colon Delimited
- Tab Delimited
- Tilde Delimited

Essentially, the only differences in the code is how the delimiter is used, but the code examples are also going to show you how the information can be arranged in both Horizontal and Vertical Views.

Colon Delimited Horizontal View

```
Set ws = CreateObject("WScript.Shell")
Set fso = CreateObject("Scripting.FileSystemObject")
Set txtstream =fso.OpenTextFile(ws.CurrentDirectory + "\Products.txt", 2, true, -2)
tstr= ""
For x = 0 to rs.Fields.Count-1
   if tstr <> """" Then
      tstr = tstr + ":"
   End If
   tstr = tstr + rs.Fields(x).Name
Next
txtstream.Writeline(tstr)
tstr = ""
rs.MoveFirst()
Do While(rs.EOF = false)
   For x = 0 to rs.Fields.Count-1
      if tstr <> """" Then
         tstr = tstr + ":"
      End If
      tstr = tstr + chr(34) + rs.Fields(x).Value + chr(34)
   Next
   txtstream.Writeline(tstr)
   tstr = ""
   rs.MoveNext
Loop
```

Colon Delimited Vertical View

```
For x = 0 to rs.Fields.Count-1
   tstr = rs.Fields(x).Name
```

```
        rs.MoveFirst()
        Do While(rs.EOF = false)
           if tstr <> "" Then
              tstr = tstr + ":"
           End If
           tstr = tstr + chr(34) + rs.Fields(x).Value + chr(34)
           rs.MoveNext
        Loop
        txtstream.Writeline(tstr)
        tstr = ""
     Next
     txtstream.Close
```

Comma Delimited Horizontal

```
     Set ws = CreateObject("WScript.Shell")
     Set fso = CreateObject("Scripting.FileSystemObject")
     Set txtstream =fso.OpenTextFile(ws.CurrentDirectory + "\Products.csv", 2, true, -2)
        tstr= ""
        For x = 0 to rs.Fields.Count-1
           if tstr <> "" Then
              tstr = tstr + ","
           End If
           tstr = tstr + rs.Fields(x).Name
        Next
        txtstream.Writeline(tstr)
        tstr = ""
        rs.MoveFirst()
        Do While(rs.EOF = false)
           For x = 0 to rs.Fields.Count-1
              if tstr <> "" Then
```

```
            tstr = tstr + ","
        End If
        tstr = tstr + chr(34) + rs.Fields(x).Value + chr(34)
    Next
    txtstream.Writeline(tstr)
    tstr = ""
    rs.MoveNext
Loop
```

Comma Delimited Vertical

```
    Set ws = CreateObject("WScript.Shell")
    Set fso = CreateObject("Scripting.FileSystemObject")
    Set txtstream =fso.OpenTextFile(ws.CurrentDirectory + "\Products.csv", 2, true, -2)

    For x = 0 to rs.Fields.Count-1
        tstr = rs.Fields(x).Name
        rs.MoveFirst()
        Do While(rs.EOF = false)
            if tstr <> """ Then
                tstr = tstr + ","
            End If
            tstr = tstr + chr(34) + rs.Fields(x).Value + chr(34)
            rs.MoveNext
        Loop
        txtstream.Writeline(tstr)
        tstr = ""
    Next
    txtstream.Close
```

Exclamation Delimited Horizontal

```
Set ws = CreateObject("WScript.Shell")
Set fso = CreateObject("Scripting.FileSystemObject")
Set txtstream =fso.OpenTextFile(ws.CurrentDirectory + "\Products.txt", 2, true, -2)
tstr= ""
For x = 0 to rs.Fields.Count-1
   if tstr <> "" Then
      tstr = tstr + "!"
   End If
   tstr = tstr + rs.Fields(x).Name
Next
txtstream.Writeline(tstr)
tstr = ""
rs.MoveFirst()
Do While(rs.EOF = false)
   For x = 0 to rs.Fields.Count-1
      if tstr <> "" Then
         tstr = tstr + "!"
      End If
      tstr = tstr + chr(34) + rs.Fields(x).Value + chr(34)
   Next
   txtstream.Writeline(tstr)
   tstr = ""
   rs.MoveNext
Loop
```

Exclamation Delimited Vertical

```
Set ws = CreateObject("WScript.Shell")
```

```
Set fso = CreateObject("Scripting.FileSystemObject")
Set txtstream =fso.OpenTextFile(ws.CurrentDirectory + "\Products.txt", 2, true, -2)

    For x = 0 to rs.Fields.Count-1
       tstr = rs.Fields(x).Name
       rs.MoveFirst()
       Do While(rs.EOF = false)
          if tstr <> "" Then
             tstr = tstr + "!"
          End If
          tstr = tstr + chr(34) + rs.Fields(x).Value + chr(34)
          rs.MoveNext
       Loop
       txtstream.Writeline(tstr)
       tstr = ""
    Next
    txtstream.Close
```

Semi Colon Delimited Horizontal

```
Set ws = CreateObject("WScript.Shell")
Set fso = CreateObject("Scripting.FileSystemObject")
Set txtstream =fso.OpenTextFile(ws.CurrentDirectory + "\Products.txt", 2, true, -2)
    tstr= ""
    For x = 0 to rs.Fields.Count-1
       if tstr <> "" Then
          tstr = tstr + ";"
       End If
       tstr = tstr + rs.Fields(x).Name
    Next
```

```
        txtstream.Writeline(tstr)
        tstr = ""
        rs.MoveFirst()
        Do While(rs.EOF = false)
            For x = 0 to rs.Fields.Count-1
                if tstr <> "" Then
                    tstr = tstr + ";"
                End If
                tstr = tstr + chr(34) + rs.Fields(x).Value + chr(34)
            Next
            txtstream.Writeline(tstr)
            tstr = ""
            rs.MoveNext
        Loop
```

Semi Colon Delimited Vertical

```
        Set ws = CreateObject("WScript.Shell")
        Set fso = CreateObject("Scripting.FileSystemObject")
        Set txtstream =fso.OpenTextFile(ws.CurrentDirectory + "\Products.txt", 2, true, -2)

        For x = 0 to rs.Fields.Count-1
            tstr = rs.Fields(x).Name
            rs.MoveFirst()
            Do While(rs.EOF = false)
                if tstr <> "" Then
                    tstr = tstr + ";"
                End If
                tstr = tstr + chr(34) + rs.Fields(x).Value + chr(34)
                rs.MoveNext
            Loop
            txtstream.Writeline(tstr)
```

```
        tstr = ""
    Next
    txtstream.Close
```

Tab Delimited Horizontal

```
    Set ws = CreateObject("WScript.Shell")
    Set fso = CreateObject("Scripting.FileSystemObject")
    Set txtstream =fso.OpenTextFile(ws.CurrentDirectory + "\Products.txt", 2, true, -2)
    tstr= ""

    For x = 0 to rs.Fields.Count-1
       if tstr <> """ Then
          tstr = tstr + vbTab
       End If
       tstr = tstr + rs.Fields(x).Name
    Next
    txtstream.Writeline(tstr)
    tstr = ""
    rs.MoveFirst()
    Do While(rs.EOF = false)
       For x = 0 to rs.Fields.Count-1
          if tstr <> """ Then
             tstr = tstr + vbTab
          End If
          tstr = tstr + chr(34) + rs.Fields(x).Value + chr(34)
       Next
       txtstream.Writeline(tstr)
       tstr = ""
       rs.MoveNext
    Loop
```

Tab Delimited Vertical

```
Set ws = CreateObject("WScript.Shell")
Set fso = CreateObject("Scripting.FileSystemObject")
Set txtstream =fso.OpenTextFile(ws.CurrentDirectory + "\Products.txt", 2, true, -2)

For x = 0 to rs.Fields.Count-1
    tstr = rs.Fields(x).Name
    rs.MoveFirst()
    Do While(rs.EOF = false)
       if tstr <> "" Then
          tstr = tstr + vbTab
       End If
       tstr = tstr + chr(34) + rs.Fields(x).Value + chr(34)
       rs.MoveNext
    Loop
    txtstream.Writeline(tstr)
    tstr = ""
Next
txtstream.Close
```

Tilde Delimited Horizontal

```
Set ws = CreateObject("WScript.Shell")
Set fso = CreateObject("Scripting.FileSystemObject")
Set txtstream =fso.OpenTextFile(ws.CurrentDirectory + "\Products.txt", 2, true, -2)
    tstr= ""
    For x = 0 to rs.Fields.Count-1
```

```
            if tstr <> "" Then
                tstr = tstr + "~"
            End If
            tstr = tstr + rs.Fields(x).Name
        Next
        txtstream.Writeline(tstr)
        tstr = ""
        rs.MoveFirst()
        Do While(rs.EOF = false)
            For x = 0 to rs.Fields.Count-1
                if tstr <> "" Then
                    tstr = tstr + "~"
                End If
                tstr = tstr + chr(34) + rs.Fields(x).Value + chr(34)
            Next
            txtstream.Writeline(tstr)
            tstr = ""
            rs.MoveNext
        Loop
```

Tilde Delimited Vertical

```
        Set ws = CreateObject("WScript.Shell")
        Set fso = CreateObject("Scripting.FileSystemObject")
        Set txtstream =fso.OpenTextFile(ws.CurrentDirectory + "\Products.txt", 2, true, -2)
        For x = 0 to rs.Fields.Count-1
            tstr = rs.Fields(x).Name
            rs.MoveFirst()
            Do While(rs.EOF = false)
                if tstr <> "" Then
                    tstr = tstr + "~"
```

```
        End If
        tstr = tstr + chr(34) + rs.Fields(x).Value + chr(34)
        rs.MoveNext
    Loop
    txtstream.Writeline(tstr)
    tstr = ""
Next
txtstream.Close
```

XML Files

In this section of the book, we're going to be Coding for the creation of Attribute XML Element XML, Element XML for XSL and Schema XML

Attribute XML Using A Text file

```
ws  = CreateObject("WScript.Shell")
fso = CreateObject("Scripting.FileSystemObject")
txtstream = fso.OpenTextFile("C:\Products.xml", 2, true, -2)
txtstream.WriteLine("<?xml version='1.0' encoding='iso-8859-1'?>")
txtstream.WriteLine("<data>")
rs.MoveFirst()
Do While(rs.EOF = false)
    txtstream.WriteLine("<Products>")
    For x in range(rs.Fields.Count):
        txtstream.WriteLine("<property name = """ + rs.Fields(x).Name + """ value=""" + rs.Fields(x).value + """/>")
    Next
    txtstream.WriteLine("</Products>")
    rs.MoveNext()
Loop
```

txtstream.WriteLine("</data>")
txtstream.Close

Attribute XML Using the DOM

```
    Set xmldoc = CreateObject("MSXML2.DOMDocument")
    Set pi = xmldoc.CreateProcessingInstruction("xml", "version='1.0' encoding='ISO-8859-1'")
    Set oRoot = xmldoc.CreateElement("data")
    xmldoc.AppendChild(pi)
    Do While rs.EOF = false
      Set oNode = xmldoc.CreateNode(1, "Products", "")
      for x in range(rs.Fields.Count):
        Set oNode1 = xmldoc.CreateNode(1, "Property", "")
        Set oAtt = xmldoc.CreateAttribute("NAME")
        oAtt.Value = rs.Fields(x).Name
        oNode1.Attributes.SetNamedItem(oAtt)
        Set oAtt = xmldoc.CreateAttribute("DATATYPE")
        oAtt.Value = str(rs.Fields(x).Type.Name))
        oNode1.Attributes.SetNamedItem(oAtt)
        Set oAtt = xmldoc.CreateAttribute("SIZE")
        oAtt.Value = str(rs.Fields(x).Value.)
        oNode1.Attributes.SetNamedItem(oAtt)
        Set oAtt = xmldoc.CreateAttribute("Value")
        oAtt.Value = GetValue(prop, obj)
        oNode1.Attributes.SetNamedItem(oAtt)
        oNode.AppendChild(oNode1)
      Next
      oRoot.AppendChild(oNode)
    Loop
    xmldoc.AppendChild(oRoot)
```

```
Set ws = CreateObject("WScript.Shell")
xmldoc.Save(ws.CurrentDirectory + "\\Products.xml")
```

Element XML Using A Text file

```
Set ws = CreateObject("WScript.Shell")
Set fso = CreateObject("Scripting.FileSystemObject")
Set txtstream =fso.OpenTextFile(ws.CurrentDirectory + "\Products.txt", 2, true, -2)
txtstream.WriteLine("<?xml version='1.0' encoding='iso-8859-1'?>")
txtstream.WriteLine("<data>")
rs.MoveFirst
Do While(rs.EOF = false)
    txtstream.WriteLine("<Products>")
    For x = 0 to rs.Fields.Count-1
        txtstream.WriteLine("<" + rs.Fields(x).Name + ">" + rs.Fields(x).Value + "</" + rs.Fields(x).Name + ">")
    Next
    txtstream.WriteLine("</Products>")
    rs.MoveNext()
Loop
txtstream.WriteLine("</data>")
txtstream.close()
```

Element XML Using the DOM

```
Set xmldoc = CreateObject("MSXML2.DOMDocument")
Set pi = xmldoc.CreateProcessingInstruction("xml", "version='1.0' encoding='ISO-8859-1'")
```

```
Set oRoot = xmldoc.CreateElement("data")
xmldoc.AppendChild(pi)
Do While rs.EOF = false
    Set oNode = xmldoc.CreateNode(1, "Products", "")
    for x = 0 to rs.Fields.Count -1
        Set oNode1 = xmldoc.CreateNode(1, rs.Fields(x),Name, "")
        oNode1.Text = str(rs.Fields(x).Value)
        Call oNode.AppendChild(oNode1)
    Next
    Call oRoot.AppendChild(oNode)
    rs.MoveNext
Loop
Call xmldoc.AppendChild(oRoot)
Set ws = CreateObject("WScript.Shell")
xmldoc.Save(ws.CurrentDirectory + "\\Products.xml")
```

Element XML FOR XSL Using A Text File

```
Set ws = CreateObject("WScript.Shell")
Set fso = CreateObject("Scripting.FileSystemObject")
Set txtstream =fso.OpenTextFile(ws.CurrentDirectory + "\Products.txt", 2, true, -2)
    txtstream.WriteLine("<?xml version='1.0' encoding='iso-8859-1'?>")
    txtstream.WriteLine("<?xml-stylesheet    type='Text/xsl'    href='" + ws.CurrentDirectory + "\Products.xsl"?>
    txtstream.WriteLine("<?xml version='1.0' encoding='iso-8859-1'?>")
    txtstream.WriteLine("<data>")
    rs.MoveFirst
    Do While(rs.EOF = false)
        txtstream.WriteLine("<Products>")
        For x = 0 to rs.Fields.Count-1
            txtstream.WriteLine("<" + rs.Fields(x).Name + ">" + rs.Fields(x).Value + "</" + rs.Fields(x).Name + ">")
```

```
    Next
    txtstream.WriteLine("</Products>")
    rs.MoveNext()
Loop
txtstream.WriteLine("</data>")
txtstream.close()
```

Element XML FOR XSL Using The DOM

```
    Set xmldoc = CreateObject("MSXML2.DOMDocument")
    Set  pi  =  xmldoc.CreateProcessingInstruction("xml",  "version='1.0'
encoding='ISO-8859-1'")
    Set   pii   =   xmldoc.CreateProcessingInstruction("xml-stylesheet",
"type='text/xsl' href='Process.xsl'")
    Set oRoot = xmldoc.CreateElement("data")
    xmldoc.AppendChild(pi)
    xmldoc.AppendChild(pii)
    Do While rs.EOF = false
      Set oNode = xmldoc.CreateNode(1, "Products", "")
      for x = 0 to rs.Fields.Count -1
        Set oNode1 = xmldoc.CreateNode(1, rs.Fields(x),Name, "")
        oNode1.Text = str(rs.Fields(x).Value)
        Call oNode.AppendChild(oNode1)
      Next
      Call oRoot.AppendChild(oNode)
      rs.MoveNext
    Loop
    Call xmldoc.AppendChild(oRoot)
    Set ws = CreateObject("WScript.Shell")
    xmldoc.Save(ws.CurrentDirectory + "\\Products.xml")
```

Schema XML Using A Text File

```
        Set ws = CreateObject("WScript.Shell")
        Set fso = CreateObject("Scripting.FileSystemObject")
        Set txtstream =fso.OpenTextFile(ws.CurrentDirectory + "\Products.txt", 2, true, -2)
        txtstream.WriteLine("<?xml version='1.0' encoding='iso-8859-1'?>")
        txtstream.WriteLine("<data>")
        rs.MoveFirst
        Do While(rs.EOF = false)
           txtstream.WriteLine("<Products>")
           For x = 0 to rs.Fields.Count-1
              txtstream.WriteLine("<" + rs.Fields(x).Name + ">" + rs.Fields(x).Value + "</" + rs.Fields(x).Name + ">")
           Next
           txtstream.WriteLine("</Products>")
           rs.MoveNext()
        Loop
        txtstream.WriteLine("</data>")
        txtstream.close()
        rs1 = CreateObject("ADODB.Recordset")
        rs1.ActiveConnection           =           "Provider=MSDAOSP; Data Source=msxml2.DSOControl"
        rs1.Open(ws.CurrentDirectory + "\Products.xml")

        If (fso.FileExists(ws.CurrentDirectory + "\Products_Schema.xml") = true) Then
            fso.DeleteFile(ws.CurrentDirectory + "\Products_Schema.xml")


        rs.Save(ws.CurrentDirectory + "\Products_Schema.xml", 1)
```

Schema XML Using the DOM

```
    Set xmldoc = CreateObject("MSXML2.DOMDocument")
    Set pi = xmldoc.CreateProcessingInstruction("xml", "version='1.0'
encoding='ISO-8859-1'")
    Set oRoot = xmldoc.CreateElement("data")
    xmldoc.AppendChild(pi)
    Do While rs.EOF = false
       Set oNode = xmldoc.CreateNode(1, "Products", "")
       for x = 0 to rs.Fields.Count -1
            Set oNode1 = xmldoc.CreateNode(1, rs.Fields(x),Name, "")
            oNode1.Text = str(rs.Fields(x).Value)
            Call oNode.AppendChild(oNode1)
       Next
       Call oRoot.AppendChild(oNode)
       rs.MoveNext
    Loop
    Call xmldoc.AppendChild(oRoot)
    Set ws = CreateObject("WScript.Shell")
    xmldoc.Save(ws.CurrentDirectory + "\\Products.xml")



    rs1 = CreateObject("ADODB.Recordset")
    rs1.ActiveConnection = "Provider=MSDAOSP; Data
Source=msxml2.DSOControl"
    rs1.Open(ws.CurrentDirectory + "\Products.xml")

    If (fso.FileExists(ws.CurrentDirectory + "\Products_Schema.xml") = true)
Then
         fso.DeleteFile(ws.CurrentDirectory + "\Products_Schema.xml")


    rs.Save(ws.CurrentDirectory + "\Products_Schema.xml", 1)
```

Excel Coding Examples

BELOW ARE SOME EXAMPLES OF ADO DRIVING EXCEL VISUAL RENDERINGS.

Excel Code in Horizontal Format using a CSV File

```
    Set ws = CreateObject("WScript.Shell")
    Set fso = CreateObject("Scripting.FileSystemObject")
    Set txtstream =fso.OpenTextFile(ws.CurrentDirectory + "\Products.csv", 2, true, -2)
    tstr= ""


    For x = 0 to rs.Fields.Count-1
      if tstr <> "" Then
         tstr = tstr + ","
      End If
      tstr = tstr + rs.Fields(x).Name
    Next
    txtstream.Writeline(tstr)
    tstr = ""
    rs.MoveFirst()
    Do While(rs.EOF = false)
```

```
        For x = 0 to rs.Fields.Count-1
          if tstr <> "" Then
            tstr = tstr + ","
          End If
          tstr = tstr + chr(34) + rs.Fields(x).Value + chr(34)
        Next
        txtstream.Writeline(tstr)
        tstr = ""
        rs.MoveNext
     Loop
```

Excel Code in Vertical Format using a CSV File

```
     Set ws = CreateObject("WScript.Shell")
     Set fso = CreateObject("Scripting.FileSystemObject")
     Set txtstream =fso.OpenTextFile(ws.CurrentDirectory + "\Products.csv", 2, true, -2)
     tstr= ""
     For x = 0 to rs.Fields.Count-1
        tstr = rs.Fields(x).Name
        rs.MoveFirst()
        Do While(rs.EOF = false)
          if tstr <> "" Then
            tstr = tstr + ","
          End If
          tstr = tstr + chr(34) + rs.Fields(x).Value + chr(34)
          rs.MoveNext
        Loop
        txtstream.Writeline(tstr)
        tstr = ""
     Next
     txtstream.Close
```

```
ws.Run(ws.CurrentDirectory + "\Products.csv")
```

Excel using Horizontal Format Automation Code

```
Set oExcel = CreateObject("Excel.Application")
oExcel.Visible = true
Set wb = oExcel.Workbooks.Add()
Set ws = wb.WorkSheets(1)
ws.Name = "Products"
y=2
For x = 0 to rs.Fields.Count-1
   ws.Cells.Item(1, x+1) = rs.Fields(x).Name
Next
rs.MoveFirst()
Do While rs.EOF = False
  For x = 0 to rs.Fields.Count-1
     ws.Cells.Item(y, x +1) = rs.Fields(x).Value
  Next
  y=y+1
  rs.MoveNext
Loop

ws.Columns.HorizontalAlignment = -4131
iret = ws.Columns.AutoFit()
```

Excel using Vertical Format Automation Code

```
oExcel = CreateObject("Excel.Application")
oExcel.Visible = true
wb = oExcel.Workbooks.Add()
Set ws = wb.WorkSheets(1)
ws.Name = "Products"
```

```
y=2
For x = 0 to rs.Fields.Count-1
   ws.Cells.Item(x+1, 1) = rs.Fields(x).Name
Next
rs.MoveFirst()
Do While rs.EOF = False
   For x = 0 to rs.Fields.Count-1
      ws.Cells.Item(x +1, y) = rs.Fields(x).Value
   Next
   y=y+1
   rs.MoveNext
Loop


ws.Columns.HorizontalAlignment = -4131
iret = ws.Columns.AutoFit()
```

Excel Spreadsheet Example

```
Set ws = CreateObject("WScript.Shell")
Set fso = CreateObject("Scripting.FileSystemObject")
Set txtstream =fso.OpenTextFile(ws.CurrentDirectory + "\\ProcessExcel.xml", 2, true, -2)
txtstream.WriteLine("<?xml version='1.0'?>")
txtstream.WriteLine("<?mso-application progid='Excel.Sheet'?>")
txtstream.WriteLine("<Workbook      xmlns='urn:schemas-microsoft-com:office:spreadsheet'      xmlns:o='urn:schemas-microsoft-com:office:office' xmlns:x='urn:schemas-microsoft-com:office:excel'      xmlns:ss='urn:schemas-microsoft-com:office:spreadsheet'      xmlns:html='http://www.w3.org/TR/REC-html40'>")
txtstream.WriteLine("   <DocumentProperties    xmlns='urn:schemas-microsoft-com:office:office'>")
```

```
txtstream.WriteLine("                    <Author>Windows User</Author>")
txtstream.WriteLine("                    <LastAuthor>Windows User</LastAuthor>")
txtstream.WriteLine("                    <Created>2007-11-27T19:36:16Z</Created>")
txtstream.WriteLine("                    <Version>12.00</Version>")
txtstream.WriteLine("             </DocumentProperties>")
txtstream.WriteLine("             <ExcelWorkbook                xmlns='urn:schemas-microsoft-com:office:excel'>")
txtstream.WriteLine("                 <WindowHeight>11835</WindowHeight>")
txtstream.WriteLine("                 <WindowWidth>18960</WindowWidth>")
txtstream.WriteLine("                    <WindowTopX>120</WindowTopX>")
txtstream.WriteLine("                    <WindowTopY>135</WindowTopY>")
txtstream.WriteLine("                 <ProtectStructure>False</ProtectStructure>")
txtstream.WriteLine("                 <ProtectWindows>False</ProtectWindows>")
txtstream.WriteLine("             </ExcelWorkbook>")
txtstream.WriteLine("             <Styles>")
txtstream.WriteLine("                  <Style            ss:ID='Default' ss:Name='Normal'>")
txtstream.WriteLine("                        <Alignment ss:Vertical='Bottom'/>")
txtstream.WriteLine("                        <Borders/>")
txtstream.WriteLine("                        <Font   ss:FontName='Calibri' x:Family='Swiss' ss:Size='11' ss:Color='#000000'/>")
txtstream.WriteLine("                        <Interior/>")
txtstream.WriteLine("                        <NumberFormat/>")
txtstream.WriteLine("                        <Protection/>")
txtstream.WriteLine("                   </Style>")
txtstream.WriteLine("                   <Style ss:ID='s62'>")
```

```
            txtstream.WriteLine("                                <Borders/>")
            txtstream.WriteLine("                                <Font ss:FontName='Calibri' x:Family='Swiss' ss:Size='11' ss:Color='#000000' ss:Bold='1'/>")
            txtstream.WriteLine("                            </Style>")
            txtstream.WriteLine("                            <Style ss:ID='s63'>")
            txtstream.WriteLine("                                <Alignment ss:Horizontal='Left' ss:Vertical='Bottom' ss:Indent='2'/>")
            txtstream.WriteLine("                                <Font ss:FontName='Verdana' x:Family='Swiss' ss:Size='7.7' ss:Color='#000000'/>")
            txtstream.WriteLine("                            </Style>")
            txtstream.WriteLine("   </Styles>")
            txtstream.WriteLine("<Worksheet ss:Name='Process'>")
            txtstream.WriteLine("            <Table   x:FullColumns='1'   x:FullRows='1' ss:DefaultRowHeight='24.9375'>")
            txtstream.WriteLine("            <Column ss:AutoFitWidth='1' ss:Width='82.5' ss:Span='5'/>")
            txtstream.WriteLine("      <Row ss:AutoFitHeight='0'>")
            For x = 0 To rs.Fields.Count-1
                txtstream.WriteLine("                              <Cell ss:StyleID='s62'><Data ss:Type='String'>" + rs.Fields(x).Name + "</Data></Cell>")
            Next
            txtstream.WriteLine("     </Row>")
            Do While rs.EOF = false
                txtstream.WriteLine("      <Row ss:AutoFitHeight='0' ss:Height='13.5'>")
                For x = 0 To rs.Fields.Count-1
                    txtstream.WriteLine("          <Cell><Data ss:Type='String'><!(CDATA(" + str(rs.Fields(x).Value)) + "))></Data></Cell>")
                Next
                txtstream.WriteLine("      </Row>")
                rs.MoveNext()
            Loop
            txtstream.WriteLine("  </Table>")
```

```
        txtstream.WriteLine("            <WorksheetOptions         xmlns='urn:schemas-microsoft-com:office:excel'>")
        txtstream.WriteLine("                <PageSetup>")
        txtstream.WriteLine("                    <Header x:Margin='0.3'/>")
        txtstream.WriteLine("                    <Footer x:Margin='0.3'/>")
        txtstream.WriteLine("                    <PageMargins x:Bottom='0.75' x:Left='0.7' x:Right='0.7' x:Top='0.75'/>")
        txtstream.WriteLine("                </PageSetup>")
        txtstream.WriteLine("                <Unsynced/>")
        txtstream.WriteLine("                <Print>")
        txtstream.WriteLine("                    <FitHeight>0</FitHeight>")
        txtstream.WriteLine("                    <ValidPrinterInfo/>")
        txtstream.WriteLine("                    <HorizontalResolution>600</HorizontalResolution>")
        txtstream.WriteLine("                    <VerticalResolution>600</VerticalResolution>")
        txtstream.WriteLine("                </Print>")
        txtstream.WriteLine("                <Selected/>")
        txtstream.WriteLine("                <Panes>")
        txtstream.WriteLine("                    <Pane>")
        txtstream.WriteLine("                        <Number>3</Number>")
        txtstream.WriteLine("                        <ActiveRow>9</ActiveRow>")
        txtstream.WriteLine("                        <ActiveCol>7</ActiveCol>")
        txtstream.WriteLine("                    </Pane>")
        txtstream.WriteLine("                </Panes>")
        txtstream.WriteLine("                <ProtectObjects>False</ProtectObjects>")
        txtstream.WriteLine("                <ProtectScenarios>False</ProtectScenarios>")
        txtstream.WriteLine("            </WorksheetOptions>")
```

```
txtstream.WriteLine("</Worksheet>")
txtstream.WriteLine("</Workbook>")
txtstream.Close()
ws.Run(ws.CurrentDirectory + "\\Products.xml")
```

Creating XSL Files

BELOW are examples of creating XSL files.

```
Set ws = CreateObject("WScript.Shell")
Set fso = CreateObject("Scripting.FileSystemObject")
Set  txtstream =fso.OpenTextFile(ws.CurrentDirectory + "\Products.xsl", 2, true, -2)
txtstream.WriteLine("<?xml version='1.0' encoding='UTF-8'?>")
txtstream.WriteLine("<xsl:stylesheet                         version='1.0' xmlns:xsl='http://www.w3.org/1999/XSL/Transform'>")
txtstream.WriteLine("<xsl:template match=""/"">")
txtstream.WriteLine("<html>")
txtstream.WriteLine("<head>")
txtstream.WriteLine("<title>Products</title>")
txtstream.WriteLine("</head>")
#Add Stylesheet Here
txtstream.WriteLine("<body>")
rs.MoveFirst()
```

Single Line Horizontal Reports

```
txtstream.WriteLine("<table border='0' Cellpadding='2' cellspacing='2>")

    txtstream.WriteLine("<tr>")
    for x = 0 to rs.Fields.count-1
        txtstream.WriteLine("<th align='left' nowrap='true'>" + rs.Fields(x).Name + "</th>")
    Next
    txtstream.WriteLine("</tr>")
    txtstream.WriteLine("<tr>")
    for x = 0 to rs.Fields.count-1
```

NONE

```
        txtstream.WriteLine("<td><xsl:value-of    select=""data/Products/" + rs.Fields(x).Name + """/></td>")
```

BUTTON

```
        txtstream.WriteLine("<td    align='left'    nowrap='true'><button style='width:100%;'><xsl:value-of select=""data/Products/" + rs.Fields(x).Name + """/></button></td>")
```

COMBOBOX

```
        txtstream.WriteLine("<td    align='left' nowrap='true'><select><option><xsl:attribute    name='value'><xsl:value-of select=""data/Products/" + rs.Fields(x).Name + """/></xsl:attribute><xsl:value-of select=""data/Products/" + rs.Fields(x).Name + """/></option></select></td>")
```

DIV

txtstream.WriteLine("<td align='left' nowrap='true'> <xsl:value-of select=""data/Products/" + rs.Fields(x).Name + """/> </td>")

LINK

txtstream.WriteLine("<td align='left' nowrap='true'><a href='" + rs.Fields(x).Value + "'><xsl:value-of select=""data/Products/" + rs.Fields(x).Name + """/></a></td>")

LISTBOX

txtstream.WriteLine("<td align='left' nowrap='true'><select multiple><option><xsl:attribute name='value'><xsl:value-of select=""data/Products/" + rs.Fields(x).Name + """/></xsl:attribute><xsl:value-of select=""data/Products/" + rs.Fields(x).Name + """/></option></select></td>")

SPAN

txtstream.WriteLine("<td align='left' nowrap='true'><xsl:value-of select=""data/Products/" + rs.Fields(x).Name + """/></td>")

TEXTAREA

txtstream.WriteLine("<td align='left' nowrap='true'><textarea><xsl:value-of select=""data/Products/" + rs.Fields(x).Name + """/></textarea></td>")

TEXTBOX

txtstream.WriteLine("<td align='left' nowrap='true'><input type='text'><xsl:attribute name=""value""><xsl:value-of select=""data/Products/" + rs.Fields(x).Name + """/></xsl:attribute></input></td>")
Next
txtstream.WriteLine("</tr>")
txtstream.WriteLine("</table>")
txtstream.WriteLine("</body>")
txtstream.WriteLine("</html>")
txtstream.WriteLine("</xsl:template>")
txtstream.WriteLine("</xsl:stylesheet>")
txtstream.Close()

Multi Line Horizontal Reports

txtstream.WriteLine("<table border='0' Cellpadding='2' cellspacing='2>")

txtstream.WriteLine("<tr>")
for x = 0 to rs.Fields.count-1
    txtstream.WriteLine("<th>" + rs.Fields(x).Name + "</th>")
Next
txtstream.WriteLine("</tr>")
txtstream.WriteLine("<xsl:for-each select=""data/Products"">")
txtstream.WriteLine("<tr>")
for x = 0 to rs.Fields.count-1
    txtstream.WriteLine("<td><xsl:value-of select="" " + rs.Fields(x).Name + " ""/></td>")

NONE

txtstream.WriteLine("<td><xsl:value-of select=""" + rs.Fields(x).Name + """/></td>")

BUTTON

txtstream.WriteLine("<td align='left' nowrap='true'><button style='width:100%;'><xsl:value-of select=""" + rs.Fields(x).Name + """/></button></td>")

COMBOBOX

txtstream.WriteLine("<td align='left' nowrap='true'><select><option><xsl:attribute name='value'><xsl:value-of select=""" + rs.Fields(x).Name + """/></xsl:attribute><xsl:value-of select=""data/Products/" + rs.Fields(x).Name + """/></option></select></td>")

DIV

txtstream.WriteLine("<td align='left' nowrap='true'> <xsl:value-of select=""data/Products/" + rs.Fields(x).Name + """/> </td>")

LINK

txtstream.WriteLine("<td align='left' nowrap='true'><a href='" + rs.Fields(x).Value + "'><xsl:value-of select=""data/Products/" + rs.Fields(x).Name + """/></a></td>")

LISTBOX

txtstream.WriteLine("<td align='left' nowrap='true'><select multiple><option><xsl:attribute name='value'><xsl:value-of select=""data/Products/" + rs.Fields(x).Name + """/></xsl:attribute><xsl:value-of select=""data/Products/" + rs.Fields(x).Name + """/></option></select></td>")

SPAN

txtstream.WriteLine("<td align='left' nowrap='true'><xsl:value-of select=""data/Products/" + rs.Fields(x).Name + """/></td>")

TEXTAREA

txtstream.WriteLine("<td align='left' nowrap='true'><textarea><xsl:value-of select=""data/Products/" + rs.Fields(x).Name + """/></textarea></td>")

TEXTBOX

txtstream.WriteLine("<td align='left' nowrap='true'><input type='text'><xsl:attribute name=""value""><xsl:value-of select=""data/Products/" + rs.Fields(x).Name + """/></xsl:attribute></input></td>")
        Next
        txtstream.WriteLine("</tr>")
        txtstream.WriteLine("</xsl:for-each>")
        txtstream.WriteLine("</table>")
        txtstream.WriteLine("</body>")
        txtstream.WriteLine("</html>")
        txtstream.WriteLine("</xsl:template>")
        txtstream.WriteLine("</xsl:stylesheet>")
        txtstream.Close()

Single Line Vertical Reports

```
for x = 0 to rs.Fields.count-1
    txtstream.WriteLine("<tr><th>" + rs.Fields(x).Name + "</th>")
```

NONE

```
txtstream.WriteLine("<td><xsl:value-of select=""data/Products/" + rs.Fields(x).Name + """/></td></tr>")
```

BUTTON

```
txtstream.WriteLine("<td align='left' nowrap='true'><button style='width:100%;'><xsl:value-of select=""data/Products/" + rs.Fields(x).Name + """/></button></td></tr>")
```

COMBOBOX

```
txtstream.WriteLine("<td align='left' nowrap='true'><select><option><xsl:attribute name='value'><xsl:value-of select=""data/Products/" + rs.Fields(x).Name + """/></xsl:attribute><xsl:value-of select=""data/Products/" + rs.Fields(x).Name + """/></option></select></td></tr>")
```

DIV

```
txtstream.WriteLine("<td align='left' nowrap='true'><div><xsl:value-of select=""data/Products/" + rs.Fields(x).Name + """/></div></td></tr>")
```

LINK

```
txtstream.WriteLine("<td align='left' nowrap='true'><a href='" + rs.Fields(x).Value + "'><xsl:value-of select=""data/Products/" + rs.Fields(x).Name + """/></a></td></tr>")
```

LISTBOX

txtstream.WriteLine("<td align='left' nowrap='true'><select multiple><option><xsl:attribute name='value'><xsl:value-of select=""data/Products/" + rs.Fields(x).Name + """/></xsl:attribute><xsl:value-of select=""data/Products/" + rs.Fields(x).Name + """/></option></select></td></tr>")

SPAN

txtstream.WriteLine("<td align='left' nowrap='true'><xsl:value-of select=""data/Products/" + rs.Fields(x).Name + """/></td></tr>")

TEXTAREA

txtstream.WriteLine("<td align='left' nowrap='true'><textarea><xsl:value-of select=""data/Products/" + rs.Fields(x).Name + """/></textarea></td></tr>")

TEXTBOX

txtstream.WriteLine("<td align='left' nowrap='true'><input type='text'><xsl:attribute name=""value""><xsl:value-of select=""data/Products/" + rs.Fields(x).Name + """/></xsl:attribute></input></td></tr>")

    Next
    txtstream.WriteLine("</table>")
    txtstream.WriteLine("</body>")
    txtstream.WriteLine("</html>")
    txtstream.WriteLine("</xsl:template>")
    txtstream.WriteLine("</xsl:stylesheet>")

txtstream.Close()

Multi Line Vertical Reports

txtstream.WriteLine("<table border='0' Cellpadding='2' cellspacing='2>")

```
for x = 0 to rs.Fields.count-1
    txtstream.WriteLine("<tr><th align='left' nowrap='true'>" + rs.Fields(x).Name + "</th>")
```

NONE

txtstream.WriteLine("<xsl:for-each select=""data/Products""><td align='left' nowrap='true'><xsl:value-of select=""" + rs.Fields(x).Name + """/></td></xsl:for-each></tr>")

BUTTON

txtstream.WriteLine("<xsl:for-each select=""data/Products""><td align='left' nowrap='true'><button style='width:100%;'><xsl:value-of select=""" + rs.Fields(x).Name + """/></button></td></xsl:for-each></tr>")

COMBOBOX

txtstream.WriteLine("<xsl:for-each select=""data/Products""><td align='left' nowrap='true'><select><option><xsl:attribute name='value'><xsl:value-of select=""" + rs.Fields(x).Name +

""""/></xsl:attribute><xsl:value-of select=""""data/Products/"" + rs.Fields(x).Name + """"/></option></select></td></xsl:for-each></tr>")

DIV

txtstream.WriteLine("<xsl:for-each select=""""data/Products""""><td align='left' nowrap='true'> <xsl:value-of select=""""data/Products/"" + rs.Fields(x).Name + """"/> </td></xsl:for-each></tr>")

LINK

txtstream.WriteLine("<xsl:for-each select=""""data/Products""""><td align='left' nowrap='true'><a href='" + rs.Fields(x).Value + "'><xsl:value-of select=""""data/Products/"" + rs.Fields(x).Name + """"/></a></td></xsl:for-each></tr>")

LISTBOX

txtstream.WriteLine("<xsl:for-each select=""""data/Products""""><td align='left' nowrap='true'><select multiple><option><xsl:attribute name='value'><xsl:value-of select=""""data/Products/"" + rs.Fields(x).Name + """"/></xsl:attribute><xsl:value-of select=""""data/Products/"" + rs.Fields(x).Name + """"/></option></select></td></xsl:for-each></tr>")

SPAN

txtstream.WriteLine("<xsl:for-each select=""""data/Products""""><td align='left' nowrap='true'><xsl:value-of select=""""data/Products/"" + rs.Fields(x).Name + """"/></td></xsl:for-each></tr>")

TEXTAREA

```
            txtstream.WriteLine("<xsl:for-each        select=""data/Products""><td
align='left'   nowrap='true'><textarea><xsl:value-of   select=""data/Products/"   +
rs.Fields(x).Name + """/></textarea></td></xsl:for-each></tr>")
```

TEXTBOX

```
            txtstream.WriteLine("<xsl:for-each        select=""data/Products""><td
align='left'           nowrap='true'><input           type='text'><xsl:attribute
name=""value""><xsl:value-of  select=""data/Products/"  +  rs.Fields(x).Name   +
"""/></xsl:attribute></input></td></xsl:for-each></tr>")
```

```
        Next
        txtstream.WriteLine("</table>")
        txtstream.WriteLine("</body>")
        txtstream.WriteLine("</html>")
        txtstream.WriteLine("</xsl:template>")
        txtstream.WriteLine("</xsl:stylesheet>")
        txtstream.Close()
```

Single Line Horizontal Tables

```
        txtstream.WriteLine("<table     style='border:Double;border-width:1px;border-
color:navy;' rules=all frames=both cellpadding=2 cellspacing=2 Width=0>")


        txtstream.WriteLine("<tr>")
        for x = 0 to rs.Fields.count-1
            txtstream.WriteLine("<th align='left' nowrap='true'>" + rs.Fields(x).Name
+ "</th>")

        txtstream.WriteLine("</tr>")
```

```
txtstream.WriteLine("<tr>")
for x = 0 to rs.Fields.count-1
```

NONE

```
txtstream.WriteLine("<td><xsl:value-of select=""data/Products/" + rs.Fields(x).Name + """/></td>")
```

BUTTON

```
txtstream.WriteLine("<td align='left' nowrap='true'><button style='width:100%;'><xsl:value-of select=""data/Products/" + rs.Fields(x).Name + """/></button></td>")
```

COMBOBOX

```
txtstream.WriteLine("<td align='left' nowrap='true'><select><option><xsl:attribute name='value'><xsl:value-of select=""data/Products/" + rs.Fields(x).Name + """/></xsl:attribute><xsl:value-of select=""data/Products/" + rs.Fields(x).Name + """/></option></select></td>")
```

DIV

```
txtstream.WriteLine("<td align='left' nowrap='true'><div><xsl:value-of select=""data/Products/" + rs.Fields(x).Name + """/></div></td>")
```

LINK

```
txtstream.WriteLine("<td align='left' nowrap='true'><a href='" + rs.Fields(x).Value + "'><xsl:value-of select=""data/Products/" + rs.Fields(x).Name + """/></a></td>")
```

LISTBOX

txtstream.WriteLine("<td align='left' nowrap='true'><select multiple><option><xsl:attribute name='value'><xsl:value-of select=""data/Products/" + rs.Fields(x).Name + """/></xsl:attribute><xsl:value-of select=""data/Products/" + rs.Fields(x).Name + """/></option></select></td>")

SPAN

txtstream.WriteLine("<td align='left' nowrap='true'><xsl:value-of select=""data/Products/" + rs.Fields(x).Name + """/></td>")

TEXTAREA

txtstream.WriteLine("<td align='left' nowrap='true'><textarea><xsl:value-of select=""data/Products/" + rs.Fields(x).Name + """/></textarea></td>")

TEXTBOX

txtstream.WriteLine("<td align='left' nowrap='true'><input type='text'><xsl:attribute name=""value""><xsl:value-of select=""data/Products/" + rs.Fields(x).Name + """/></xsl:attribute></input></td>")

Next
txtstream.WriteLine("</tr>")
txtstream.WriteLine("</table>")
txtstream.WriteLine("</body>")
txtstream.WriteLine("</html>")

txtstream.WriteLine("</xsl:template>")
txtstream.WriteLine("</xsl:stylesheet>")
txtstream.Close()

Multi Line Horizontal Tables

txtstream.WriteLine("<table style='border:Double;border-width:1px;border-color:navy;' rules=all frames=both cellpadding=2 cellspacing=2 Width=0>")

txtstream.WriteLine("<tr>")
for x = 0 to rs.Fields.count-1
    txtstream.WriteLine("<th>" + rs.Fields(x).Name + "</th>")
Next
txtstream.WriteLine("</tr>")
txtstream.WriteLine("<xsl:for-each select=""data/Products"">")
txtstream.WriteLine("<tr>")
for x = 0 to rs.Fields.count-1
    txtstream.WriteLine("<td><xsl:value-of select="" " + rs.Fields(x).Name + " ""/></td>")

NONE

txtstream.WriteLine("<td><xsl:value-of select=""" + rs.Fields(x).Name + """/></td>")

BUTTON

txtstream.WriteLine("<td align='left' nowrap='true'><button style='width:100%;'><xsl:value-of select=""" + rs.Fields(x).Name + """/></button></td>")

COMBOBOX

txtstream.WriteLine("<td align='left' nowrap='true'><select><option><xsl:attribute name='value'><xsl:value-of select=""" + rs.Fields(x).Name + """/></xsl:attribute><xsl:value-of select=""""data/Products/" + rs.Fields(x).Name + """/></option></select></td>")

DIV

txtstream.WriteLine("<td align='left' nowrap='true'> <xsl:value-of select=""""data/Products/" + rs.Fields(x).Name + """/> </td>")

LINK

txtstream.WriteLine("<td align='left' nowrap='true'><a href='" + rs.Fields(x).Value + "'><xsl:value-of select=""""data/Products/" + rs.Fields(x).Name + """/></a></td>")

LISTBOX

txtstream.WriteLine("<td align='left' nowrap='true'><select multiple><option><xsl:attribute name='value'><xsl:value-of select=""""data/Products/" + rs.Fields(x).Name + """/></xsl:attribute><xsl:value-of select=""""data/Products/" + rs.Fields(x).Name + """/></option></select></td>")

SPAN

txtstream.WriteLine("<td align='left' nowrap='true'><xsl:value-of select=""""data/Products/" + rs.Fields(x).Name + """/></td>")

TEXTAREA

txtstream.WriteLine("<td align='left' nowrap='true'><textarea><xsl:value-of select=""data/Products/" + rs.Fields(x).Name + """/></textarea></td>")

TEXTBOX

txtstream.WriteLine("<td align='left' nowrap='true'><input type='text'><xsl:attribute name=""value""><xsl:value-of select=""data/Products/" + rs.Fields(x).Name + """/></xsl:attribute></input></td>")

Next
txtstream.WriteLine("</tr>")
txtstream.WriteLine("</xsl:for-each>")
txtstream.WriteLine("</table>")
txtstream.WriteLine("</body>")
txtstream.WriteLine("</html>")
txtstream.WriteLine("</xsl:template>")
txtstream.WriteLine("</xsl:stylesheet>")
txtstream.Close()

Single Line Vertical Tables

for x = 0 to rs.Fields.count-1
    txtstream.WriteLine("<tr><th>" + rs.Fields(x).Name + "</th>")

NONE

txtstream.WriteLine("<td><xsl:value-of select=""data/Products/" + rs.Fields(x).Name + """/></td></tr>")

BUTTON

txtstream.WriteLine("<td align='left' nowrap='true'><button style='width:100%;'><xsl:value-of select=""data/Products/" + rs.Fields(x).Name + """/></button></td></tr>")

COMBOBOX

txtstream.WriteLine("<td align='left' nowrap='true'><select><option><xsl:attribute name='value'><xsl:value-of select=""data/Products/" + rs.Fields(x).Name + """/></xsl:attribute><xsl:value-of select=""data/Products/" + rs.Fields(x).Name + """/></option></select></td></tr>")

DIV

txtstream.WriteLine("<td align='left' nowrap='true'> <xsl:value-of select=""data/Products/" + rs.Fields(x).Name + """/> </td></tr>")

LINK

txtstream.WriteLine("<td align='left' nowrap='true'><a href='" + rs.Fields(x).Value + "'><xsl:value-of select=""data/Products/" + rs.Fields(x).Name + """/></a></td></tr>")

LISTBOX

txtstream.WriteLine("<td align='left' nowrap='true'><select multiple><option><xsl:attribute name='value'><xsl:value-of

select=""data/Products/" + rs.Fields(x).Name + """/></xsl:attribute><xsl:value-of select=""data/Products/" + rs.Fields(x).Name + """/></option></select></td></tr>")

SPAN

txtstream.WriteLine("<td align='left' nowrap='true'><xsl:value-of select=""data/Products/" + rs.Fields(x).Name + """/></td></tr>")

TEXTAREA

txtstream.WriteLine("<td align='left' nowrap='true'><textarea><xsl:value-of select=""data/Products/" + rs.Fields(x).Name + """/></textarea></td></tr>")

TEXTBOX

txtstream.WriteLine("<td align='left' nowrap='true'><input type='text'><xsl:attribute name=""value""><xsl:value-of select=""data/Products/" + rs.Fields(x).Name + """/></xsl:attribute></input></td></tr>")

Next
txtstream.WriteLine("</table>")
txtstream.WriteLine("</body>")
txtstream.WriteLine("</html>")
txtstream.WriteLine("</xsl:template>")
txtstream.WriteLine("</xsl:stylesheet>")
txtstream.Close()

Multi Line Vertical Tables

txtstream.WriteLine("<table style='border:Double;border-width:1px;border-color:navy;' rules=all frames=both cellpadding=2 cellspacing=2 Width=0>")

for x = 0 to rs.Fields.count-1
txtstream.WriteLine("<tr><th align='left' nowrap='true'>" + rs.Fields(x).Name + "</th>")

NONE

txtstream.WriteLine("<xsl:for-each select=""data/Products""><td align='left' nowrap='true'><xsl:value-of select=""" + rs.Fields(x).Name + """/></td></xsl:for-each></tr>")

BUTTON

txtstream.WriteLine("<xsl:for-each select=""data/Products""><td align='left' nowrap='true'><button style='width:100%;'><xsl:value-of select=""" + rs.Fields(x).Name + """/></button></td></xsl:for-each></tr>")

COMBOBOX

txtstream.WriteLine("<xsl:for-each select=""data/Products""><td align='left' nowrap='true'><select><option><xsl:attribute name='value'><xsl:value-of select=""" + rs.Fields(x).Name + """/></xsl:attribute><xsl:value-of select=""data/Products/" + rs.Fields(x).Name + """/></option></select></td></xsl:for-each></tr>")

DIV

txtstream.WriteLine("<xsl:for-each select=""data/Products""><td align='left' nowrap='true'> <xsl:value-of select=""data/Products/" + rs.Fields(x).Name + """/> </td></xsl:for-each></tr>")

LINK

txtstream.WriteLine("<xsl:for-each select=""data/Products""><td align='left' nowrap='true'><a href='" + rs.Fields(x).Value + "'><xsl:value-of select=""data/Products/" + rs.Fields(x).Name + """/></a></td></xsl:for-each></tr>")

LISTBOX

txtstream.WriteLine("<xsl:for-each select=""data/Products""><td align='left' nowrap='true'><select multiple><option><xsl:attribute name='value'><xsl:value-of select=""data/Products/" + rs.Fields(x).Name + """/></xsl:attribute><xsl:value-of select=""data/Products/" + rs.Fields(x).Name + """/></option></select></td></xsl:for-each></tr>")

SPAN

txtstream.WriteLine("<xsl:for-each select=""data/Products""><td align='left' nowrap='true'><xsl:value-of select=""data/Products/" + rs.Fields(x).Name + """/></td></xsl:for-each></tr>")

TEXTAREA

txtstream.WriteLine("<xsl:for-each select=""data/Products""><td align='left' nowrap='true'><textarea><xsl:value-of select=""data/Products/" + rs.Fields(x).Name + """/></textarea></td></xsl:for-each></tr>")

TEXTBOX

```
            txtstream.WriteLine("<xsl:for-each     select=""data/Products""><td
align='left'          nowrap='true'><input          type='text'><xsl:attribute
name=""value""><xsl:value-of select=""data/Products/" + rs.Fields(x).Name    +
"""/></xsl:attribute></input></td></xsl:for-each></tr>")

    Next
    txtstream.WriteLine("</table>")
    txtstream.WriteLine("</body>")
    txtstream.WriteLine("</html>")
    txtstream.WriteLine("</xsl:template>")
    txtstream.WriteLine("</xsl:stylesheet>")
    txtstream.Close()
```

Stylesheets
Add some Pizzazz To your ASP, HTA, HTML and XSL pages

CSS turns okay into Amazing

BELOW is an assortment of stylesheets. There is nothing spectacular about them Just some ideas you can modify and put your own twist on them.

None

```
txtstream.WriteLine("<style type='text/css'>")
txtstream.WriteLine("th")
txtstream.WriteLine("{")
txtstream.WriteLine("   COLOR: Black;")
txtstream.WriteLine("}")
txtstream.WriteLine("td")
txtstream.WriteLine("{")
txtstream.WriteLine("   COLOR: Black;")
txtstream.WriteLine("}")
txtstream.WriteLine("</style>")
```

Its A Table

```
        txtstream.WriteLine("<style type='text/css'>")
        txtstream.WriteLine("#itsthetable {")
        txtstream.WriteLine("      font-family: Georgia, ""Times New Roman"", Times, serif;")
        txtstream.WriteLine("      color: #036;")
        txtstream.WriteLine("}")
        txtstream.WriteLine("caption {")
        txtstream.WriteLine("      font-size: 48px;")
        txtstream.WriteLine("      color: #036;")
        txtstream.WriteLine("      font-weight: bolder;")
        txtstream.WriteLine("      font-variant: small-caps;")
        txtstream.WriteLine("}")
        txtstream.WriteLine("th {")
        txtstream.WriteLine("      font-size: 12px;")
        txtstream.WriteLine("      color: #FFF;")
        txtstream.WriteLine("      background-color: #06C;")
        txtstream.WriteLine("      padding: 8px 4px;")
        txtstream.WriteLine("      border-bottom: 1px solid #015ebc;")
        txtstream.WriteLine("}")
        txtstream.WriteLine("table {")
        txtstream.WriteLine("      margin: 0;")
        txtstream.WriteLine("      padding: 0;")
        txtstream.WriteLine("      border-collapse: collapse;")
        txtstream.WriteLine("      border: 1px solid #06C;")
        txtstream.WriteLine("      width: 100%")
        txtstream.WriteLine("}")
        txtstream.WriteLine("#itsthetable th a:link, #itsthetable th a:visited {")
        txtstream.WriteLine("      color: #FFF;")
        txtstream.WriteLine("      text-decoration: none;")
        txtstream.WriteLine("      border-left: 5px solid #FFF;")
```

```
            txtstream.WriteLine("        padding-left: 3px;")
            txtstream.WriteLine("}")
            txtstream.WriteLine("th a:hover, #itsthetable th a:active {")
            txtstream.WriteLine("        color: #F90;")
            txtstream.WriteLine("        text-decoration: line-through;")
            txtstream.WriteLine("        border-left: 5px solid #F90;")
            txtstream.WriteLine("        padding-left: 3px;")
            txtstream.WriteLine("}")
            txtstream.WriteLine("tbody th:hover {")
            txtstream.WriteLine("        background-image: url(imgs/tbody_hover.gif);")
            txtstream.WriteLine("        background-position: bottom;")
            txtstream.WriteLine("        background-repeat: repeat-x;")
            txtstream.WriteLine("}")
            txtstream.WriteLine("td {")
            txtstream.WriteLine("        background-color: #f2f2f2;")
            txtstream.WriteLine("        padding: 4px;")
            txtstream.WriteLine("        font-size: 12px;")
            txtstream.WriteLine("}")
            txtstream.WriteLine("#itsthetable td:hover {")
            txtstream.WriteLine("        background-color: #f8f8f8;")
            txtstream.WriteLine("}")
            txtstream.WriteLine("#itsthetable td a:link, #itsthetable td a:visited {")
            txtstream.WriteLine("        color: #039;")
            txtstream.WriteLine("        text-decoration: none;")
            txtstream.WriteLine("        border-left: 3px solid #039;")
            txtstream.WriteLine("        padding-left: 3px;")
            txtstream.WriteLine("}")
            txtstream.WriteLine("#itsthetable td a:hover, #itsthetable td a:active {")
            txtstream.WriteLine("        color: #06C;")
            txtstream.WriteLine("        text-decoration: line-through;")
            txtstream.WriteLine("        border-left: 3px solid #06C;")
            txtstream.WriteLine("        padding-left: 3px;")
```

```
txtstream.WriteLine("}")
txtstream.WriteLine("#itsthetable th {")
txtstream.WriteLine("     text-align: left;")
txtstream.WriteLine("     width: 150px;")
txtstream.WriteLine("}")
txtstream.WriteLine("#itsthetable tr {")
txtstream.WriteLine("     border-bottom: 1px solid #CCC;")
txtstream.WriteLine("}")
txtstream.WriteLine("#itsthetable thead th {")
txtstream.WriteLine("     background-image: url(imgs/thead_back.gif);")
txtstream.WriteLine("     background-repeat: repeat-x;")
txtstream.WriteLine("     background-color: #06C;")
txtstream.WriteLine("     height: 30px;")
txtstream.WriteLine("     font-size: 18px;")
txtstream.WriteLine("     text-align: center;")
txtstream.WriteLine("     text-shadow: #333 2px 2px;")
txtstream.WriteLine("     border: 2px;")
txtstream.WriteLine("}")
txtstream.WriteLine("#itsthetable tfoot th {")
txtstream.WriteLine("     background-image: url(imgs/tfoot_back.gif);")
txtstream.WriteLine("     background-repeat: repeat-x;")
txtstream.WriteLine("     background-color: #036;")
txtstream.WriteLine("     height: 30px;")
txtstream.WriteLine("     font-size: 28px;")
txtstream.WriteLine("     text-align: center;")
txtstream.WriteLine("     text-shadow: #333 2px 2px;")
txtstream.WriteLine("}")
txtstream.WriteLine("#itsthetable tfoot td {")
txtstream.WriteLine("     background-image: url(imgs/tfoot_back.gif);")
txtstream.WriteLine("     background-repeat: repeat-x;")
txtstream.WriteLine("     background-color: #036;")
txtstream.WriteLine("     color: FFF;")
txtstream.WriteLine("     height: 30px;")
```

```
txtstream.WriteLine("        font-size: 24px;")
txtstream.WriteLine("        text-align: left;")
txtstream.WriteLine("        text-shadow: #333 2px 2px;")
txtstream.WriteLine("}")
txtstream.WriteLine("tbody td a(href=""http://www.csslab.cl/"") {")
txtstream.WriteLine("        font-weight: bolder;")
txtstream.WriteLine("}")
txtstream.WriteLine("</style>")
```

Black and White Text

```
txtstream.WriteLine("<style type='text/css'>")
txtstream.WriteLine("th")
txtstream.WriteLine("{")
txtstream.WriteLine("   COLOR: white;")
txtstream.WriteLine("   BACKGROUND-COLOR: black;")
txtstream.WriteLine("   FONT-FAMILY: Cambria, serif;")
txtstream.WriteLine("   FONT-SIZE: 12px;")
txtstream.WriteLine("   text-align: left;")
txtstream.WriteLine("   white-Space: nowrap='nowrap';")
txtstream.WriteLine("}")
txtstream.WriteLine("td")
txtstream.WriteLine("{")
txtstream.WriteLine("   COLOR: white;")
txtstream.WriteLine("   BACKGROUND-COLOR: black;")
txtstream.WriteLine("   FONT-FAMILY: font-family: Cambria, serif;")
txtstream.WriteLine("   FONT-SIZE: 12px;")
txtstream.WriteLine("   text-align: left;")
txtstream.WriteLine("   white-Space: nowrap='nowrap';")
txtstream.WriteLine("}")
txtstream.WriteLine("div")
txtstream.WriteLine("{")
txtstream.WriteLine("   COLOR: white;")
```

```
txtstream.WriteLine("    BACKGROUND-COLOR: black;")
txtstream.WriteLine("    FONT-FAMILY: font-family: Cambria, serif;")
txtstream.WriteLine("    FONT-SIZE: 10px;")
txtstream.WriteLine("    text-align: left;")
txtstream.WriteLine("    white-Space: nowrap='nowrap';")
txtstream.WriteLine("}")
txtstream.WriteLine("span")
txtstream.WriteLine("{")
txtstream.WriteLine("    COLOR: white;")
txtstream.WriteLine("    BACKGROUND-COLOR: black;")
txtstream.WriteLine("    FONT-FAMILY: font-family: Cambria, serif;")
txtstream.WriteLine("    FONT-SIZE: 10px;")
txtstream.WriteLine("    text-align: left;")
txtstream.WriteLine("    white-Space: nowrap='nowrap';")
txtstream.WriteLine("    display:inline-block;")
txtstream.WriteLine("    width: 100%;")
txtstream.WriteLine("}")
txtstream.WriteLine("textarea")
txtstream.WriteLine("{")
txtstream.WriteLine("    COLOR: white;")
txtstream.WriteLine("    BACKGROUND-COLOR: black;")
txtstream.WriteLine("    FONT-FAMILY: font-family: Cambria, serif;")
txtstream.WriteLine("    FONT-SIZE: 10px;")
txtstream.WriteLine("    text-align: left;")
txtstream.WriteLine("    white-Space: nowrap='nowrap';")
txtstream.WriteLine("    width: 100%;")
txtstream.WriteLine("}")
txtstream.WriteLine("select")
txtstream.WriteLine("{")
txtstream.WriteLine("    COLOR: white;")
txtstream.WriteLine("    BACKGROUND-COLOR: black;")
txtstream.WriteLine("    FONT-FAMILY: font-family: Cambria, serif;")
txtstream.WriteLine("    FONT-SIZE: 10px;")
```

```
txtstream.WriteLine("    text-align: left;")
txtstream.WriteLine("    white-Space: nowrap='nowrap';")
txtstream.WriteLine("    width: 100%;")
txtstream.WriteLine("}")
txtstream.WriteLine("input")
txtstream.WriteLine("{")
txtstream.WriteLine("    COLOR: white;")
txtstream.WriteLine("    BACKGROUND-COLOR: black;")
txtstream.WriteLine("    FONT-FAMILY: font-family: Cambria, serif;")
txtstream.WriteLine("    FONT-SIZE: 12px;")
txtstream.WriteLine("    text-align: left;")
txtstream.WriteLine("    display:table-cell;")
txtstream.WriteLine("    white-Space: nowrap='nowrap';")
txtstream.WriteLine("}")
txtstream.WriteLine("h1 {")
txtstream.WriteLine("color: antiquewhite;")
txtstream.WriteLine("text-shadow: 1px 1px 1px black;")
txtstream.WriteLine("padding: 3px;")
txtstream.WriteLine("text-align: center;")
txtstream.WriteLine("box-shadow: in2px 2px 5px rgba(0,0,0,0.5), in-2px -2px 5px rgba(255,255,255,0.5);")
txtstream.WriteLine("}")
txtstream.WriteLine("</style>")
```

Colored Text

```
txtstream.WriteLine("<style type='text/css'>")
txtstream.WriteLine("th")
txtstream.WriteLine("{")
txtstream.WriteLine("    COLOR: darkred;")
txtstream.WriteLine("    BACKGROUND-COLOR: #eeeeee;")
txtstream.WriteLine("    FONT-FAMILY: Cambria, serif;")
txtstream.WriteLine("    FONT-SIZE: 12px;")
```

```
txtstream.WriteLine("    text-align: left;")
txtstream.WriteLine("    white-Space: nowrap='nowrap';")
txtstream.WriteLine("}")
txtstream.WriteLine("td")
txtstream.WriteLine("{")
txtstream.WriteLine("    COLOR: navy;")
txtstream.WriteLine("    BACKGROUND-COLOR: #eeeeee;")
txtstream.WriteLine("    FONT-FAMILY: font-family: Cambria, serif;")
txtstream.WriteLine("    FONT-SIZE: 12px;")
txtstream.WriteLine("    text-align: left;")
txtstream.WriteLine("    white-Space: nowrap='nowrap';")
txtstream.WriteLine("}")
txtstream.WriteLine("div")
txtstream.WriteLine("{")
txtstream.WriteLine("    COLOR: white;")
txtstream.WriteLine("    BACKGROUND-COLOR: navy;")
txtstream.WriteLine("    FONT-FAMILY: font-family: Cambria, serif;")
txtstream.WriteLine("    FONT-SIZE: 10px;")
txtstream.WriteLine("    text-align: left;")
txtstream.WriteLine("    white-Space: nowrap='nowrap';")
txtstream.WriteLine("}")
txtstream.WriteLine("span")
txtstream.WriteLine("{")
txtstream.WriteLine("    COLOR: white;")
txtstream.WriteLine("    BACKGROUND-COLOR: navy;")
txtstream.WriteLine("    FONT-FAMILY: font-family: Cambria, serif;")
txtstream.WriteLine("    FONT-SIZE: 10px;")
txtstream.WriteLine("    text-align: left;")
txtstream.WriteLine("    white-Space: nowrap='nowrap';")
txtstream.WriteLine("    display:inline-block;")
txtstream.WriteLine("    width: 100%;")
txtstream.WriteLine("}")
txtstream.WriteLine("textarea")
```

txtstream.WriteLine("{")
txtstream.WriteLine("   COLOR: white;")
txtstream.WriteLine("   BACKGROUND-COLOR: navy;")
txtstream.WriteLine("   FONT-FAMILY: font-family: Cambria, serif;")
txtstream.WriteLine("   FONT-SIZE: 10px;")
txtstream.WriteLine("   text-align: left;")
txtstream.WriteLine("   white-Space: nowrap='nowrap';")
txtstream.WriteLine("   width: 100%;")
txtstream.WriteLine("}")
txtstream.WriteLine("select")
txtstream.WriteLine("{")
txtstream.WriteLine("   COLOR: white;")
txtstream.WriteLine("   BACKGROUND-COLOR: navy;")
txtstream.WriteLine("   FONT-FAMILY: font-family: Cambria, serif;")
txtstream.WriteLine("   FONT-SIZE: 10px;")
txtstream.WriteLine("   text-align: left;")
txtstream.WriteLine("   white-Space: nowrap='nowrap';")
txtstream.WriteLine("   width: 100%;")
txtstream.WriteLine("}")
txtstream.WriteLine("input")
txtstream.WriteLine("{")
txtstream.WriteLine("   COLOR: white;")
txtstream.WriteLine("   BACKGROUND-COLOR: navy;")
txtstream.WriteLine("   FONT-FAMILY: font-family: Cambria, serif;")
txtstream.WriteLine("   FONT-SIZE: 12px;")
txtstream.WriteLine("   text-align: left;")
txtstream.WriteLine("   display:table-cell;")
txtstream.WriteLine("   white-Space: nowrap='nowrap';")
txtstream.WriteLine("}")
txtstream.WriteLine("h1 {")
txtstream.WriteLine("color: antiquewhite;")
txtstream.WriteLine("text-shadow: 1px 1px 1px black;")
txtstream.WriteLine("padding: 3px;")

txtstream.WriteLine("text-align: center;")
txtstream.WriteLine("box-shadow: in2px 2px 5px rgba(0,0,0,0.5), in-2px -2px 5px rgba(255,255,255,0.5);")
txtstream.WriteLine("}")
txtstream.WriteLine("</style>")

Oscillating Row Colors

txtstream.WriteLine("<style type='text/css'>")
txtstream.WriteLine("th")
txtstream.WriteLine("{")
txtstream.WriteLine("   COLOR: white;")
txtstream.WriteLine("   BACKGROUND-COLOR: navy;")
txtstream.WriteLine("   FONT-FAMILY: Cambria, serif;")
txtstream.WriteLine("   FONT-SIZE: 12px;")
txtstream.WriteLine("   text-align: left;")
txtstream.WriteLine("   white-Space: nowrap='nowrap';")
txtstream.WriteLine("}")
txtstream.WriteLine("td")
txtstream.WriteLine("{")
txtstream.WriteLine("   COLOR: navy;")
txtstream.WriteLine("   FONT-FAMILY: font-family: Cambria, serif;")
txtstream.WriteLine("   FONT-SIZE: 12px;")
txtstream.WriteLine("   text-align: left;")
txtstream.WriteLine("   white-Space: nowrap='nowrap';")
txtstream.WriteLine("}")
txtstream.WriteLine("div")
txtstream.WriteLine("{")
txtstream.WriteLine("   COLOR: navy;")
txtstream.WriteLine("   FONT-FAMILY: font-family: Cambria, serif;")
txtstream.WriteLine("   FONT-SIZE: 12px;")
txtstream.WriteLine("   text-align: left;")
txtstream.WriteLine("   white-Space: nowrap='nowrap';")

```
txtstream.WriteLine("}")
txtstream.WriteLine("span")
txtstream.WriteLine("{")
txtstream.WriteLine("    COLOR: navy;")
txtstream.WriteLine("    FONT-FAMILY: font-family: Cambria, serif;")
txtstream.WriteLine("    FONT-SIZE: 12px;")
txtstream.WriteLine("    text-align: left;")
txtstream.WriteLine("    white-Space: nowrap='nowrap';")
txtstream.WriteLine("    width: 100%;")
txtstream.WriteLine("}")
txtstream.WriteLine("textarea")
txtstream.WriteLine("{")
txtstream.WriteLine("    COLOR: navy;")
txtstream.WriteLine("    FONT-FAMILY: font-family: Cambria, serif;")
txtstream.WriteLine("    FONT-SIZE: 12px;")
txtstream.WriteLine("    text-align: left;")
txtstream.WriteLine("    white-Space: nowrap='nowrap';")
txtstream.WriteLine("    display:inline-block;")
txtstream.WriteLine("    width: 100%;")
txtstream.WriteLine("}")
txtstream.WriteLine("select")
txtstream.WriteLine("{")
txtstream.WriteLine("    COLOR: navy;")
txtstream.WriteLine("    FONT-FAMILY: font-family: Cambria, serif;")
txtstream.WriteLine("    FONT-SIZE: 10px;")
txtstream.WriteLine("    text-align: left;")
txtstream.WriteLine("    white-Space: nowrap='nowrap';")
txtstream.WriteLine("    display:inline-block;")
txtstream.WriteLine("    width: 100%;")
txtstream.WriteLine("}")
txtstream.WriteLine("input")
txtstream.WriteLine("{")
txtstream.WriteLine("    COLOR: navy;")
```

```
        txtstream.WriteLine("   FONT-FAMILY: font-family: Cambria, serif;")
        txtstream.WriteLine("   FONT-SIZE: 12px;")
        txtstream.WriteLine("   text-align: left;")
        txtstream.WriteLine("   display:table-cell;")
        txtstream.WriteLine("   white-Space: nowrap='nowrap';")
        txtstream.WriteLine("}")
        txtstream.WriteLine("h1 {")
        txtstream.WriteLine("color: antiquewhite;")
        txtstream.WriteLine("text-shadow: 1px 1px 1px black;")
        txtstream.WriteLine("padding: 3px;")
        txtstream.WriteLine("text-align: center;")
        txtstream.WriteLine("box-shadow: in2px 2px 5px rgba(0,0,0,0.5), in-2px -2px 5px rgba(255,255,255,0.5);")
        txtstream.WriteLine("}")
        txtstream.WriteLine("tr:nth-child(even){background-color:#f2f2f2;}")
        txtstream.WriteLine("tr:nth-child(odd){background-color:#cccccc; color:#f2f2f2;}")
        txtstream.WriteLine("</style>")
```

Ghost Decorated

```
        txtstream.WriteLine("<style type='text/css'>")
        txtstream.WriteLine("th")
        txtstream.WriteLine("{")
        txtstream.WriteLine("   COLOR: black;")
        txtstream.WriteLine("   BACKGROUND-COLOR: white;")
        txtstream.WriteLine("   FONT-FAMILY: Cambria, serif;")
        txtstream.WriteLine("   FONT-SIZE: 12px;")
        txtstream.WriteLine("   text-align: left;")
        txtstream.WriteLine("   white-Space: nowrap='nowrap';")
        txtstream.WriteLine("}")
        txtstream.WriteLine("td")
        txtstream.WriteLine("{")
```

```
txtstream.WriteLine("    COLOR: black;")
txtstream.WriteLine("    BACKGROUND-COLOR: white;")
txtstream.WriteLine("    FONT-FAMILY: font-family: Cambria, serif;")
txtstream.WriteLine("    FONT-SIZE: 12px;")
txtstream.WriteLine("    text-align: left;")
txtstream.WriteLine("    white-Space: nowrap='nowrap';")
txtstream.WriteLine("}")
txtstream.WriteLine("div")
txtstream.WriteLine("{")
txtstream.WriteLine("    COLOR: black;")
txtstream.WriteLine("    BACKGROUND-COLOR: white;")
txtstream.WriteLine("    FONT-FAMILY: font-family: Cambria, serif;")
txtstream.WriteLine("    FONT-SIZE: 10px;")
txtstream.WriteLine("    text-align: left;")
txtstream.WriteLine("    white-Space: nowrap='nowrap';")
txtstream.WriteLine("}")
txtstream.WriteLine("span")
txtstream.WriteLine("{")
txtstream.WriteLine("    COLOR: black;")
txtstream.WriteLine("    BACKGROUND-COLOR: white;")
txtstream.WriteLine("    FONT-FAMILY: font-family: Cambria, serif;")
txtstream.WriteLine("    FONT-SIZE: 10px;")
txtstream.WriteLine("    text-align: left;")
txtstream.WriteLine("    white-Space: nowrap='nowrap';")
txtstream.WriteLine("    display:inline-block;")
txtstream.WriteLine("    width: 100%;")
txtstream.WriteLine("}")
txtstream.WriteLine("textarea")
txtstream.WriteLine("{")
txtstream.WriteLine("    COLOR: black;")
txtstream.WriteLine("    BACKGROUND-COLOR: white;")
txtstream.WriteLine("    FONT-FAMILY: font-family: Cambria, serif;")
txtstream.WriteLine("    FONT-SIZE: 10px;")
```

```
txtstream.WriteLine("    text-align: left;")
txtstream.WriteLine("    white-Space: nowrap='nowrap';")
txtstream.WriteLine("    width: 100%;")
txtstream.WriteLine("}")
txtstream.WriteLine("select")
txtstream.WriteLine("{")
txtstream.WriteLine("    COLOR: black;")
txtstream.WriteLine("    BACKGROUND-COLOR: white;")
txtstream.WriteLine("    FONT-FAMILY: font-family: Cambria, serif;")
txtstream.WriteLine("    FONT-SIZE: 10px;")
txtstream.WriteLine("    text-align: left;")
txtstream.WriteLine("    white-Space: nowrap='nowrap';")
txtstream.WriteLine("    width: 100%;")
txtstream.WriteLine("}")
txtstream.WriteLine("input")
txtstream.WriteLine("{")
txtstream.WriteLine("    COLOR: black;")
txtstream.WriteLine("    BACKGROUND-COLOR: white;")
txtstream.WriteLine("    FONT-FAMILY: font-family: Cambria, serif;")
txtstream.WriteLine("    FONT-SIZE: 12px;")
txtstream.WriteLine("    text-align: left;")
txtstream.WriteLine("    display:table-cell;")
txtstream.WriteLine("    white-Space: nowrap='nowrap';")
txtstream.WriteLine("}")
txtstream.WriteLine("h1 {")
txtstream.WriteLine("color: antiquewhite;")
txtstream.WriteLine("text-shadow: 1px 1px 1px black;")
txtstream.WriteLine("padding: 3px;")
txtstream.WriteLine("text-align: center;")
txtstream.WriteLine("box-shadow: in2px 2px 5px rgba(0,0,0,0.5), in-2px -2px 5px rgba(255,255,255,0.5);")
txtstream.WriteLine("}")
txtstream.WriteLine("</style>")
```

3D

```
        txtstream.WriteLine("<style type='text/css'>")
        txtstream.WriteLine("body")
        txtstream.WriteLine("{")
        txtstream.WriteLine("   PADDING-RIGHT: 0px;")
        txtstream.WriteLine("   PADDING-LEFT: 0px;")
        txtstream.WriteLine("   PADDING-BOTTOM: 0px;")
        txtstream.WriteLine("   MARGIN: 0px;")
        txtstream.WriteLine("   COLOR: #333;")
        txtstream.WriteLine("   PADDING-TOP: 0px;")
        txtstream.WriteLine("     FONT-FAMILY: verdana, arial, helvetica, sans-serif;")
        txtstream.WriteLine("}")
        txtstream.WriteLine("table")
        txtstream.WriteLine("{")
        txtstream.WriteLine("   BORDER-RIGHT: #999999 3px solid;")
        txtstream.WriteLine("   PADDING-RIGHT: 6px;")
        txtstream.WriteLine("   PADDING-LEFT: 6px;")
        txtstream.WriteLine("   FONT-WEIGHT: Bold;")
        txtstream.WriteLine("   FONT-SIZE: 14px;")
        txtstream.WriteLine("   PADDING-BOTTOM: 6px;")
        txtstream.WriteLine("   COLOR: Peru;")
        txtstream.WriteLine("   LINE-HEIGHT: 14px;")
        txtstream.WriteLine("   PADDING-TOP: 6px;")
        txtstream.WriteLine("   BORDER-BOTTOM: #999 1px solid;")
        txtstream.WriteLine("   BACKGROUND-COLOR: #eeeeee;")
        txtstream.WriteLine("     FONT-FAMILY: verdana, arial, helvetica, sans-serif;")
        txtstream.WriteLine("   FONT-SIZE: 12px;")
        txtstream.WriteLine("}")
        txtstream.WriteLine("th")
```

```
txtstream.WriteLine("{")
txtstream.WriteLine("    BORDER-RIGHT: #999999 3px solid;")
txtstream.WriteLine("    PADDING-RIGHT: 6px;")
txtstream.WriteLine("    PADDING-LEFT: 6px;")
txtstream.WriteLine("    FONT-WEIGHT: Bold;")
txtstream.WriteLine("    FONT-SIZE: 14px;")
txtstream.WriteLine("    PADDING-BOTTOM: 6px;")
txtstream.WriteLine("    COLOR: darkred;")
txtstream.WriteLine("    LINE-HEIGHT: 14px;")
txtstream.WriteLine("    PADDING-TOP: 6px;")
txtstream.WriteLine("    BORDER-BOTTOM: #999 1px solid;")
txtstream.WriteLine("    BACKGROUND-COLOR: #eeeeee;")
txtstream.WriteLine("    FONT-FAMILY: Cambria, serif;")
txtstream.WriteLine("    FONT-SIZE: 12px;")
txtstream.WriteLine("    text-align: left;")
txtstream.WriteLine("    white-Space: nowrap='nowrap';")
txtstream.WriteLine("}")
txtstream.WriteLine(".th")
txtstream.WriteLine("{")
txtstream.WriteLine("    BORDER-RIGHT: #999999 2px solid;")
txtstream.WriteLine("    PADDING-RIGHT: 6px;")
txtstream.WriteLine("    PADDING-LEFT: 6px;")
txtstream.WriteLine("    FONT-WEIGHT: Bold;")
txtstream.WriteLine("    PADDING-BOTTOM: 6px;")
txtstream.WriteLine("    COLOR: black;")
txtstream.WriteLine("    PADDING-TOP: 6px;")
txtstream.WriteLine("    BORDER-BOTTOM: #999 2px solid;")
txtstream.WriteLine("    BACKGROUND-COLOR: #eeeeee;")
txtstream.WriteLine("    FONT-FAMILY: font-family: Cambria, serif;")
txtstream.WriteLine("    FONT-SIZE: 10px;")
txtstream.WriteLine("    text-align: right;")
txtstream.WriteLine("    white-Space: nowrap='nowrap';")
txtstream.WriteLine("}")
```

```
txtstream.WriteLine("td")
txtstream.WriteLine("{")
txtstream.WriteLine("    BORDER-RIGHT: #999999 3px solid;")
txtstream.WriteLine("    PADDING-RIGHT: 6px;")
txtstream.WriteLine("    PADDING-LEFT: 6px;")
txtstream.WriteLine("    FONT-WEIGHT: Normal;")
txtstream.WriteLine("    PADDING-BOTTOM: 6px;")
txtstream.WriteLine("    COLOR: navy;")
txtstream.WriteLine("    LINE-HEIGHT: 14px;")
txtstream.WriteLine("    PADDING-TOP: 6px;")
txtstream.WriteLine("    BORDER-BOTTOM: #999 1px solid;")
txtstream.WriteLine("    BACKGROUND-COLOR: #eeeeee;")
txtstream.WriteLine("    FONT-FAMILY: font-family: Cambria, serif;")
txtstream.WriteLine("    FONT-SIZE: 12px;")
txtstream.WriteLine("    text-align: left;")
txtstream.WriteLine("    white-Space: nowrap='nowrap';")
txtstream.WriteLine("}")
txtstream.WriteLine("div")
txtstream.WriteLine("{")
txtstream.WriteLine("    BORDER-RIGHT: #999999 3px solid;")
txtstream.WriteLine("    PADDING-RIGHT: 6px;")
txtstream.WriteLine("    PADDING-LEFT: 6px;")
txtstream.WriteLine("    FONT-WEIGHT: Normal;")
txtstream.WriteLine("    PADDING-BOTTOM: 6px;")
txtstream.WriteLine("    COLOR: white;")
txtstream.WriteLine("    PADDING-TOP: 6px;")
txtstream.WriteLine("    BORDER-BOTTOM: #999 1px solid;")
txtstream.WriteLine("    BACKGROUND-COLOR: navy;")
txtstream.WriteLine("    FONT-FAMILY: font-family: Cambria, serif;")
txtstream.WriteLine("    FONT-SIZE: 10px;")
txtstream.WriteLine("    text-align: left;")
txtstream.WriteLine("    white-Space: nowrap='nowrap';")
txtstream.WriteLine("}")
```

```
txtstream.WriteLine("span")
txtstream.WriteLine("{")
txtstream.WriteLine("    BORDER-RIGHT: #999999 3px solid;")
txtstream.WriteLine("    PADDING-RIGHT: 3px;")
txtstream.WriteLine("    PADDING-LEFT: 3px;")
txtstream.WriteLine("    FONT-WEIGHT: Normal;")
txtstream.WriteLine("    PADDING-BOTTOM: 3px;")
txtstream.WriteLine("    COLOR: white;")
txtstream.WriteLine("    PADDING-TOP: 3px;")
txtstream.WriteLine("    BORDER-BOTTOM: #999 1px solid;")
txtstream.WriteLine("    BACKGROUND-COLOR: navy;")
txtstream.WriteLine("    FONT-FAMILY: font-family: Cambria, serif;")
txtstream.WriteLine("    FONT-SIZE: 10px;")
txtstream.WriteLine("    text-align: left;")
txtstream.WriteLine("    white-Space: nowrap='nowrap';")
txtstream.WriteLine("    display:inline-block;")
txtstream.WriteLine("    width: 100%;")
txtstream.WriteLine("}")
txtstream.WriteLine("textarea")
txtstream.WriteLine("{")
txtstream.WriteLine("    BORDER-RIGHT: #999999 3px solid;")
txtstream.WriteLine("    PADDING-RIGHT: 3px;")
txtstream.WriteLine("    PADDING-LEFT: 3px;")
txtstream.WriteLine("    FONT-WEIGHT: Normal;")
txtstream.WriteLine("    PADDING-BOTTOM: 3px;")
txtstream.WriteLine("    COLOR: white;")
txtstream.WriteLine("    PADDING-TOP: 3px;")
txtstream.WriteLine("    BORDER-BOTTOM: #999 1px solid;")
txtstream.WriteLine("    BACKGROUND-COLOR: navy;")
txtstream.WriteLine("    FONT-FAMILY: font-family: Cambria, serif;")
txtstream.WriteLine("    FONT-SIZE: 10px;")
txtstream.WriteLine("    text-align: left;")
txtstream.WriteLine("    white-Space: nowrap='nowrap';")
```

```
txtstream.WriteLine("     width: 100%;")
txtstream.WriteLine("}")
txtstream.WriteLine("select")
txtstream.WriteLine("{")
txtstream.WriteLine("     BORDER-RIGHT: #999999 3px solid;")
txtstream.WriteLine("     PADDING-RIGHT: 6px;")
txtstream.WriteLine("     PADDING-LEFT: 6px;")
txtstream.WriteLine("     FONT-WEIGHT: Normal;")
txtstream.WriteLine("     PADDING-BOTTOM: 6px;")
txtstream.WriteLine("     COLOR: white;")
txtstream.WriteLine("     PADDING-TOP: 6px;")
txtstream.WriteLine("     BORDER-BOTTOM: #999 1px solid;")
txtstream.WriteLine("     BACKGROUND-COLOR: navy;")
txtstream.WriteLine("     FONT-FAMILY: font-family: Cambria, serif;")
txtstream.WriteLine("     FONT-SIZE: 10px;")
txtstream.WriteLine("     text-align: left;")
txtstream.WriteLine("     white-Space: nowrap='nowrap';")
txtstream.WriteLine("     width: 100%;")
txtstream.WriteLine("}")
txtstream.WriteLine("input")
txtstream.WriteLine("{")
txtstream.WriteLine("     BORDER-RIGHT: #999999 3px solid;")
txtstream.WriteLine("     PADDING-RIGHT: 3px;")
txtstream.WriteLine("     PADDING-LEFT: 3px;")
txtstream.WriteLine("     FONT-WEIGHT: Bold;")
txtstream.WriteLine("     PADDING-BOTTOM: 3px;")
txtstream.WriteLine("     COLOR: white;")
txtstream.WriteLine("     PADDING-TOP: 3px;")
txtstream.WriteLine("     BORDER-BOTTOM: #999 1px solid;")
txtstream.WriteLine("     BACKGROUND-COLOR: navy;")
txtstream.WriteLine("     FONT-FAMILY: font-family: Cambria, serif;")
txtstream.WriteLine("     FONT-SIZE: 12px;")
txtstream.WriteLine("     text-align: left;")
```

```
            txtstream.WriteLine("    display:table-cell;")
            txtstream.WriteLine("    white-Space: nowrap='nowrap';")
            txtstream.WriteLine("    width: 100%;")
            txtstream.WriteLine("}")
            txtstream.WriteLine("h1 {")
            txtstream.WriteLine("color: antiquewhite;")
            txtstream.WriteLine("text-shadow: 1px 1px 1px black;")
            txtstream.WriteLine("padding: 3px;")
            txtstream.WriteLine("text-align: center;")
            txtstream.WriteLine("box-shadow: in2px 2px 5px rgba(0,0,0,0.5), in-2px -2px 5px rgba(255,255,255,0.5);")
            txtstream.WriteLine("}")
            txtstream.WriteLine("</style>")
```

Shadow Box

```
            txtstream.WriteLine("<style type='text/css'>")
            txtstream.WriteLine("body")
            txtstream.WriteLine("{")
            txtstream.WriteLine("   PADDING-RIGHT: 0px;")
            txtstream.WriteLine("   PADDING-LEFT: 0px;")
            txtstream.WriteLine("   PADDING-BOTTOM: 0px;")
            txtstream.WriteLine("   MARGIN: 0px;")
            txtstream.WriteLine("   COLOR: #333;")
            txtstream.WriteLine("   PADDING-TOP: 0px;")
            txtstream.WriteLine("        FONT-FAMILY: verdana, arial, helvetica, sans-serif;")
            txtstream.WriteLine("}")
            txtstream.WriteLine("table")
            txtstream.WriteLine("{")
            txtstream.WriteLine("   BORDER-RIGHT: #999999 1px solid;")
            txtstream.WriteLine("   PADDING-RIGHT: 1px;")
            txtstream.WriteLine("   PADDING-LEFT: 1px;")
```

txtstream.WriteLine("   PADDING-BOTTOM: 1px;")
txtstream.WriteLine("   LINE-HEIGHT: 8px;")
txtstream.WriteLine("   PADDING-TOP: 1px;")
txtstream.WriteLine("   BORDER-BOTTOM: #999 1px solid;")
txtstream.WriteLine("   BACKGROUND-COLOR: #eeeeee;")
txtstream.WriteLine("   filter:progid:DXImageTransform.Microsoft.Shadow(color='silver', Direction=135, Strength=16)")
txtstream.WriteLine("}")
txtstream.WriteLine("th")
txtstream.WriteLine("{")
txtstream.WriteLine("   BORDER-RIGHT: #999999 3px solid;")
txtstream.WriteLine("   PADDING-RIGHT: 6px;")
txtstream.WriteLine("   PADDING-LEFT: 6px;")
txtstream.WriteLine("   FONT-WEIGHT: Bold;")
txtstream.WriteLine("   FONT-SIZE: 14px;")
txtstream.WriteLine("   PADDING-BOTTOM: 6px;")
txtstream.WriteLine("   COLOR: darkred;")
txtstream.WriteLine("   LINE-HEIGHT: 14px;")
txtstream.WriteLine("   PADDING-TOP: 6px;")
txtstream.WriteLine("   BORDER-BOTTOM: #999 1px solid;")
txtstream.WriteLine("   BACKGROUND-COLOR: #eeeeee;")
txtstream.WriteLine("   FONT-FAMILY: font-family: Cambria, serif;")
txtstream.WriteLine("   FONT-SIZE: 12px;")
txtstream.WriteLine("   text-align: left;")
txtstream.WriteLine("   white-Space: nowrap='nowrap';")
txtstream.WriteLine("}")
txtstream.WriteLine(".th")
txtstream.WriteLine("{")
txtstream.WriteLine("   BORDER-RIGHT: #999999 2px solid;")
txtstream.WriteLine("   PADDING-RIGHT: 6px;")
txtstream.WriteLine("   PADDING-LEFT: 6px;")
txtstream.WriteLine("   FONT-WEIGHT: Bold;")

```
txtstream.WriteLine("    PADDING-BOTTOM: 6px;")
txtstream.WriteLine("    COLOR: black;")
txtstream.WriteLine("    PADDING-TOP: 6px;")
txtstream.WriteLine("    BORDER-BOTTOM: #999 2px solid;")
txtstream.WriteLine("    BACKGROUND-COLOR: #eeeeee;")
txtstream.WriteLine("    FONT-FAMILY: font-family: Cambria, serif;")
txtstream.WriteLine("    FONT-SIZE: 10px;")
txtstream.WriteLine("    text-align: right;")
txtstream.WriteLine("    white-Space: nowrap='nowrap';")
txtstream.WriteLine("}")
txtstream.WriteLine("td")
txtstream.WriteLine("{")
txtstream.WriteLine("    BORDER-RIGHT: #999999 3px solid;")
txtstream.WriteLine("    PADDING-RIGHT: 6px;")
txtstream.WriteLine("    PADDING-LEFT: 6px;")
txtstream.WriteLine("    FONT-WEIGHT: Normal;")
txtstream.WriteLine("    PADDING-BOTTOM: 6px;")
txtstream.WriteLine("    COLOR: navy;")
txtstream.WriteLine("    LINE-HEIGHT: 14px;")
txtstream.WriteLine("    PADDING-TOP: 6px;")
txtstream.WriteLine("    BORDER-BOTTOM: #999 1px solid;")
txtstream.WriteLine("    BACKGROUND-COLOR: #eeeeee;")
txtstream.WriteLine("    FONT-FAMILY: font-family: Cambria, serif;")
txtstream.WriteLine("    FONT-SIZE: 12px;")
txtstream.WriteLine("    text-align: left;")
txtstream.WriteLine("    white-Space: nowrap='nowrap';")
txtstream.WriteLine("}")
txtstream.WriteLine("div")
txtstream.WriteLine("{")
txtstream.WriteLine("    BORDER-RIGHT: #999999 3px solid;")
txtstream.WriteLine("    PADDING-RIGHT: 6px;")
txtstream.WriteLine("    PADDING-LEFT: 6px;")
txtstream.WriteLine("    FONT-WEIGHT: Normal;")
```

```
txtstream.WriteLine("    PADDING-BOTTOM: 6px;")
txtstream.WriteLine("    COLOR: white;")
txtstream.WriteLine("    PADDING-TOP: 6px;")
txtstream.WriteLine("    BORDER-BOTTOM: #999 1px solid;")
txtstream.WriteLine("    BACKGROUND-COLOR: navy;")
txtstream.WriteLine("    FONT-FAMILY: font-family: Cambria, serif;")
txtstream.WriteLine("    FONT-SIZE: 10px;")
txtstream.WriteLine("    text-align: left;")
txtstream.WriteLine("    white-Space: nowrap='nowrap';")
txtstream.WriteLine("}")
txtstream.WriteLine("span")
txtstream.WriteLine("{")
txtstream.WriteLine("    BORDER-RIGHT: #999999 3px solid;")
txtstream.WriteLine("    PADDING-RIGHT: 3px;")
txtstream.WriteLine("    PADDING-LEFT: 3px;")
txtstream.WriteLine("    FONT-WEIGHT: Normal;")
txtstream.WriteLine("    PADDING-BOTTOM: 3px;")
txtstream.WriteLine("    COLOR: white;")
txtstream.WriteLine("    PADDING-TOP: 3px;")
txtstream.WriteLine("    BORDER-BOTTOM: #999 1px solid;")
txtstream.WriteLine("    BACKGROUND-COLOR: navy;")
txtstream.WriteLine("    FONT-FAMILY: font-family: Cambria, serif;")
txtstream.WriteLine("    FONT-SIZE: 10px;")
txtstream.WriteLine("    text-align: left;")
txtstream.WriteLine("    white-Space: nowrap='nowrap';")
txtstream.WriteLine("    display: inline-block;")
txtstream.WriteLine("    width: 100%;")
txtstream.WriteLine("}")
txtstream.WriteLine("textarea")
txtstream.WriteLine("{")
txtstream.WriteLine("    BORDER-RIGHT: #999999 3px solid;")
txtstream.WriteLine("    PADDING-RIGHT: 3px;")
txtstream.WriteLine("    PADDING-LEFT: 3px;")
```

```
txtstream.WriteLine("    FONT-WEIGHT: Normal;")
txtstream.WriteLine("    PADDING-BOTTOM: 3px;")
txtstream.WriteLine("    COLOR: white;")
txtstream.WriteLine("    PADDING-TOP: 3px;")
txtstream.WriteLine("    BORDER-BOTTOM: #999 1px solid;")
txtstream.WriteLine("    BACKGROUND-COLOR: navy;")
txtstream.WriteLine("    FONT-FAMILY: font-family: Cambria, serif;")
txtstream.WriteLine("    FONT-SIZE: 10px;")
txtstream.WriteLine("    text-align: left;")
txtstream.WriteLine("    white-Space: nowrap='nowrap';")
txtstream.WriteLine("    width: 100%;")
txtstream.WriteLine("}")
txtstream.WriteLine("select")
txtstream.WriteLine("{")
txtstream.WriteLine("    BORDER-RIGHT: #999999 3px solid;")
txtstream.WriteLine("    PADDING-RIGHT: 6px;")
txtstream.WriteLine("    PADDING-LEFT: 6px;")
txtstream.WriteLine("    FONT-WEIGHT: Normal;")
txtstream.WriteLine("    PADDING-BOTTOM: 6px;")
txtstream.WriteLine("    COLOR: white;")
txtstream.WriteLine("    PADDING-TOP: 6px;")
txtstream.WriteLine("    BORDER-BOTTOM: #999 1px solid;")
txtstream.WriteLine("    BACKGROUND-COLOR: navy;")
txtstream.WriteLine("    FONT-FAMILY: font-family: Cambria, serif;")
txtstream.WriteLine("    FONT-SIZE: 10px;")
txtstream.WriteLine("    text-align: left;")
txtstream.WriteLine("    white-Space: nowrap='nowrap';")
txtstream.WriteLine("    width: 100%;")
txtstream.WriteLine("}")
txtstream.WriteLine("input")
txtstream.WriteLine("{")
txtstream.WriteLine("    BORDER-RIGHT: #999999 3px solid;")
txtstream.WriteLine("    PADDING-RIGHT: 3px;")
```

```
            txtstream.WriteLine("    PADDING-LEFT: 3px;")
            txtstream.WriteLine("    FONT-WEIGHT: Bold;")
            txtstream.WriteLine("    PADDING-BOTTOM: 3px;")
            txtstream.WriteLine("    COLOR: white;")
            txtstream.WriteLine("    PADDING-TOP: 3px;")
            txtstream.WriteLine("    BORDER-BOTTOM: #999 1px solid;")
            txtstream.WriteLine("    BACKGROUND-COLOR: navy;")
            txtstream.WriteLine("    FONT-FAMILY: font-family: Cambria, serif;")
            txtstream.WriteLine("    FONT-SIZE: 12px;")
            txtstream.WriteLine("    text-align: left;")
            txtstream.WriteLine("    display: table-cell;")
            txtstream.WriteLine("    white-Space: nowrap='nowrap';")
            txtstream.WriteLine("    width: 100%;")
            txtstream.WriteLine("}")
            txtstream.WriteLine("h1 {")
            txtstream.WriteLine("color: antiquewhite;")
            txtstream.WriteLine("text-shadow: 1px 1px 1px black;")
            txtstream.WriteLine("padding: 3px;")
            txtstream.WriteLine("text-align: center;")
            txtstream.WriteLine("box-shadow: in2px 2px 5px rgba(0,0,0,0.5), in-2px -2px 5px rgba(255,255,255,0.5);")
            txtstream.WriteLine("}")
            txtstream.WriteLine("</style>")
```

www.ingramcontent.com/pod-product-compliance
Lightning Source LLC
Chambersburg PA
CBHW052322220526
45472CB00001B/230